**From faraway places, a Christian family story
that will be treasured in every reader's home**

INGRID TROBISCH'S

ON OUR WAY REJOICING!

with

- Her father, **Ralph Hult,** who narrowly escaped from drowning aboard the ill-fated steamer, *Zam-Zam*

- **Mother Hult** mastering Spanish at the age of fifty and serving isolated Indian villages in Bolivia

- **Ingrid** herself at her first mission in Africa, making a wedding gown on a hand-crank sewing machine

- **Veda,** who retraced her father's path in Tanganyika, as he had followed in Livingstone's footsteps

- **John** as a medical missionary and **Carl** aiding the relocation of North Korean refugees

- **All the Hults** together at their Missouri homestead for the first time in twenty years

  *...Some of the unforgettable scenes
  from this inspirational classic.*

HARPER JUBILEE BOOKS

On Our Way

Rejoicing!

INGRID HULT TROBISCH

HARPER & ROW, PUBLISHERS
New York, Hagerstown, San Francisco, London

Scripture quotations are taken from the American Standard Version and from the Revised Standard Version.

First Harper & Row Jubilee edition published in 1976.

ISBN 0-06-06-8451-8

LIBRARY OF CONGRESS CATALOG CARD NUMBER: 64-20195

76 77 78 79 80 10 9 8 7 6 5 4 3 2 1

For my children

KATHRYN, DANIEL, DAVID

STEPHEN AND RUTH

AND MY NIECES AND NEPHEWS:

May this story about your parents and grandparents help you sing with them:

> *On our way rejoicing,*
> *As we forward move,*
> *Hearken to our praises,*
> *O thou God of love!*

and pray with them:

> *God be merciful unto us, and bless us,*
> *And cause his face to shine upon us;*
> *That thy way may be known upon earth,*
> *Thy salvation among all nations.*
>
> Psalm 67:1, 2

Contents

On Our Way Rejoicing!

One.

The "Zamzam"

The long, strident ring of the class bell announced the end of the first period. Translating Caesar in our Latin II class had been an unwelcome chore indeed this May morning in 1941. As I rose from my seat, I gazed out the open window. Almost overnight the stark bareness of winter had disappeared.

Today the Academy campus lay shimmering and new, clothed in the first magic green of a Nebraska spring. I wished I were free to go out. If it weren't for tomorrow's English composition—and those finals coming up . . . Oh well, only two more weeks until the end of school. I put my books away on the shelves reserved for sophomores and then mounted the worn stairs of Old Main on my way to chapel service.

As I reached the top landing, someone called me. I turned to face our president, Dr. Paul Lindberg.

"Wait a moment, Ingrid," he said. "There's something I must tell you. Come into my office."

Without a word, I followed him. Both the tone of his voice and the troubled look on his kindly face alarmed me. Had something happened to one of my brothers and sisters? To Mother?

Suddenly, I remembered a conversation with a girl friend of mine just a few days earlier. She had asked me:

"What would be the most wonderful thing that could happen to you right now? What would be the most terrible?"

I could not remember my answer to the first question, but to the second, I recalled having said without a moment's hesitation:

"That something might happen to my father on his trip to Africa."

That must be it! Father!

Then I saw my Uncle Mart, a businessman in downtown Wahoo, waiting for us at the office door. His eyes were misty. We went in together. Dr. Lindberg told me then in quiet, deliberate words:

"We've just heard on the radio that the *Zamzam* has been sunk by a German raider. They're afraid everyone on board is lost."

The *Zamzam*! That was Daddy's ship, all right. He had sailed on it from New York to take up his post as a missionary in Tanganyika.* And we had been waiting every day for a cable telling of his safe arrival in Capetown.

The United States was not yet in the war. The *Zamzam* was a neutral ship, but she did have to sail through blockaded waters.

Father lost? Somehow, in my heart, I felt certain it wasn't true. I looked first at Uncle Mart, then at Dr. Lindberg. "Are you sure?"

They nodded. I could see by their faces that they believed it. But I couldn't—at least not yet.

Dr. Lindberg said gently:

"You're excused, Ingrid, for the rest of the day."

As I went for my books, I thought of my mother back home on the farm near Springfield, Missouri. How would she be taking the news? Then I hurried to my grandmother's house two blocks away, where I was staying for the school year.

This would be a hard blow for her. My father, her oldest son, was not the only one on the *Zamzam* who was dear to her. One of her daughters, Mrs. Einar Norberg, who was returning to Tang-

---

*Now called Tanzania.

anyika with her husband and three young children, was also aboard that ship.

As I walked up the steps to the small, white frame house, I was conscious of the inviting porch swing, the lace curtains, the potted plants in every window—the little details that did so much to make it the kind of house grandmothers are supposed to live in.

I felt a tightness in my throat as I opened the front door and stepped into the hallway onto the braided rug. A rush of memories overwhelmed me.

I was standing on the very spot where I had said good-by to my father just three months earlier.

I found Grandmother in her bedroom, sitting in her rocking chair close to the radio. The sunshine was streaming across her prized plants—I can smell the geraniums still—and lighting up her face.

She was "just being quiet," a discipline acquired with difficulty during her seventy-seven years, for she was an energetic little woman, always busy.

I noticed that her hair was still black except for some strands of gray above her temples. She was wearing her favorite lavender dress with an amethyst necklace. There were no tears in her eyes, and her face was serene.

I put my hand over hers. She responded in silent understanding. I felt that she, too, had hope. Expressions of sympathy or comfort were unnecessary.

Her words of farewell to my father came back to me. With her head barely even with his shoulders, she had looked up at him and said:

"Ralph, remember when you left for Africa that first time, more than twenty years ago? I told you then that it was the happiest day of my life. Today I want to say the same thing again."

Now the radio was telling her that she had lost not only a son but also a daughter, and all her daughter's family. Yet she could sit here calm and controlled. How I admired her!

At this moment I heard a car stop in front of the house. A man with a camera bag slung over his shoulder hurried up the steps.

"I'm from the *Herald* in Omaha," he said. "I'd like to interview Mrs. Hult, please."

I didn't want her to be disturbed. But not knowing what else to do, I introduced him to my grandmother.

"The sinking of the *Zamzam* is headline news all over the nation," he said to her. "I have here the passenger list. Is it true that you had both a son and a daughter on board?"

Grandmother nodded. She motioned him to sit down. Without a tremor, she answered his questions.

"Why did Ralph Hult want to go out to Africa when he knew it would be so dangerous?" the reporter asked.

Grandmother did not reply immediately. Instead, she got up and went to her desk.

"I have here his last letter," she said. "Let me read you a few lines:

" 'We are not going out on an adventure trip. This is a matter of urgent business for the Kingdom of God. Why should we not be confident? In giving His disciples the great commission, our Saviour assured them, "Behold, I am with you always." ' "

The reporter took a picture of the two of us sitting beside the radio anxiously waiting for more news. Then he began packing his bag.

"I've got to hurry if I'm to make the afternoon edition," he said, looking at his watch. "I've less than an hour to drive those forty miles back to Omaha."

After the reporter left, Grandmother went to get a cup of coffee. I sat looking out the window, lost in reverie. I was still thinking about the questions he had asked. I doubted that Grandmother had been able to make him understand why Father insisted on returning to Africa.

A scene that had taken place in this very house just a week before flashed into my mind. Some relatives were visiting with

Grandmother. I was doing my homework in the next room. I paid no attention to the murmur of voices until I heard the word *Zamzam*.

"I've read no news of the *Zamzam's* arrival in Capetown," a man was saying. "Wasn't it due there April 20?"

"Yes, it was," another chimed in.

"Well, today's the 10th of May. I take that as a bad sign," said a third.

"I must say," a woman remarked, "I can't understand what Gertrude was thinking of to let Ralph go—especially at a time like this. What if something happens to him? Who's going to look after her and the ten children?"

"Why, the baby isn't three yet!" exclaimed someone else. "Paul is the oldest, and even he is only a freshman in college!"

"What about Ralph's insurance?" a man asked. "How much does he have?"

"It doesn't amount to more than a thousand dollars."

"Why, that wouldn't be a drop in the bucket with all those children to be educated."

"You can talk all you want about the needy Africans," a woman declared indignantly, "but if you ask me, I think Ralph's first responsibility is to look after his own."

I couldn't believe my ears. Is that what my relatives were really thinking? I was stunned at hearing them criticize Mother for letting Father go—when all of us had been praying so long for him to get the chance.

A film I had seen recently, *Stanley and Livingstone,* was fresh in my memory. How stirring its closing moments! There, marching against a map of the Dark Continent, were pictured missionaries and hundreds of Africans all singing with resounding spirit, "Onward, Christian Soldiers." In my mind's eye I could see my father marching along with them. "Oh," I thought, "if only I were older."

I could not understand my relatives. Surely God would care

for us if anything *should* happen to Father!

My first impulse was to rush into the room and cry out at them.

But I couldn't—I was speechless. Instead, I ran into the closet under the stairs. Stumbling over the vacuum cleaner, I sat down abruptly on a pile of old *Life* magazines. In great shaking sobs, I cried until the emotion of my fifteen-year-old heart was spent. Then, to quiet myself, I began to go over in my mind the last days Father had spent with us before he left to board the *Zamzam* in New York.

I remembered chiefly how happy he was during that time. And why not? Going again to Africa was the fulfillment of a dream of fifteen years—fifteen years during which he worked as an itinerant pastor, as a peddler of books, as a laborer on a road gang, to feed his family while he waited and hoped.

How much of his life had been consumed in waiting! From boyhood he had longed to be a missionary. But he'd had to wait to get his education, wait until the call came. For a time after his marriage, his dreams began to come true. They were realized in the six years that he and Mother spent as missionaries in the Sudan and then in Tanganyika. These were the years in which brothers Paul and John and I were born, and our little sister, Ruth, whose grave was there on the slopes of Mount Kilimanjaro.

Then upon my parents' return from furlough, the mission board decided not to continue the work in the Sudan which Father had begun. There were too many difficulties, they said. Neither was he called to return to Tanganyika. He was still waiting when, after fifteen years of silence, out of the blue on a January day of this year, 1941, the letter came.

From the first paragraphs he learned what he already knew: There was great need in the mission fields of East Africa, left leaderless because so many European missionaries had been either interned or deported because of the war. The letter then went on to inquire in cautious tones whether Ralph Hult, now fifty-two years old and the father of ten, would consider returning to Tanganyika for the duration of the emergency.

Inwardly, he must have been tormented. He knew only too well what it would mean if he said yes: separation, not only from his wife, but from his growing children who needed a father. Wouldn't the price of his answering this call be too great? Yet, how could he stay at home when he had been summoned to help?

At the end of January, after consulting my mother and searching his soul, he wired his acceptance. He would be in New York by March 10 ready to sail soon thereafter. He applied for his passport and resigned from his temporary pastorate in Rapid River, Michigan. Back in Springfield he bought khaki for the tropics, mosquito nets, cooking utensils and medicines, and painted his initials "R.D.H." in neat letters on his steel foot lockers.

In February he came to Wahoo to bid us good-by—his mother, his brothers and sisters, and me, his oldest daughter.

How I loved him with the single-heartedness of a young daughter's devotion! How I admired him as I saw him walking toward me with his tall, erect figure and his purposeful stride!

His hair was gray, but it had been that way as long as I could remember, for he had seen much suffering. The wrinkles around his kind and gentle eyes made him look as if he were always smiling. Yet in the determined set of his mouth and chin there was no compromise. We children had learned early never to toy with his commands, and we were the happier for it. We never once doubted, when he was being strict with us, that it was because he loved us.

I was about to say something to my grandmother when I heard steps on the front porch. Someone entered without knocking. My Uncle Les stood there, holding a bouquet of gladiolas. Silently, with tears in his eyes, he held them out to me.

I welcomed his embrace of sympathy and loving concern, yet my heart was crying: "Why is he doing this? This is what people do when a loved one is dead. But my father is *not* dead—I know he's not. Neither are my aunt and uncle, nor my cousins, nor the other passengers aboard the *Zamzam.*"

We had to wait until noon for the next broadcast. The news was the same.

I wondered if my mother had heard it back home in Missouri. What kind of a day was she having on the farm? I thought of her, of my brothers and sisters. I could picture them going about their morning chores. It had been nine months since I left "the Homestead." That's what Father had named the place—Bethany Homestead. That name suited it better, for it wasn't much of a farm— just forty acres of trees and rocks and hills.

A wave of homesickness came over me.

All of a sudden I knew what I needed: To see them all, then go to my refuge at Lookout Point where I'd be hidden from everyone's view . . . To feel the strength of the oak tree behind me, its ragged bark digging into my back . . . To drink in the view of the rolling Ozark hills which always filled me with rejoicing, and strengthened me . . .

The woods that we loved to explore would be changing from the first delicate green of spring to the full rich green of May. Standing out against the green would be the soft lavender of the redbud trees, the rosy pink of the wild crabapple blossoms. All the fruit trees would be in bloom and their fragrance was something to dream about.

If only I could walk today over those hills, maybe my world would come straight again. If only I could talk to Mother, she would help me get my balance. But of course! I *could* talk to her. I could call her up. Why hadn't I thought of it before?

On the telephone her voice came through strong and clear. She asked first how Grandmother was taking the news. Characteristically, Mother's concern was for others. There wasn't time in those short three minutes to hear all the details of how she received the news, but this is what I learned a few weeks later when I returned home from the Academy:

"I was out hoeing the pea patch before breakfast that Monday morning," said Mother. "John and Carl were doing the milking.

Eunie had turned on the radio to listen to the seven-thirty news while she set the table and cooked the oatmeal. Then I heard her scream from the back door, 'Mother! Mother!' I put down my hoe. I did not know what to think as I watched her running toward me, her red braids flying in the wind.

" 'Mother, the *Zamzam* is sunk!' she called out. 'Everybody's drowned! They're talking about us over the radio!' I put my arm around her—she was almost hysterical—and walked with her slowly back to the house.

"By that time the five younger children had gathered in the living room. Martha was weeping, while Carl tried to comfort her and at the same time keep the tears back from his own eyes.

"Were these little ones to be left fatherless? No, I couldn't believe it. I tried to concentrate on finding out just what it was the news broadcaster had said.

"I called the radio station first, then the newspaper office. Both confirmed the report. But they were very kind and promised to keep me informed as each fresh bulletin came in.

"I sat down at the table and covered my face with my hands. I wanted to give way to grief, but I knew I must be strong for the sake of my children. I tried to console myself. What if the boat *had* been sunk? Surely, God had watched over its passengers.

"Then I gathered the children around the dining-room table. Together we read Psalm 124, that one where it says: 'If it had not been the Lord who was on our side . . . then the waters had overwhelmed us, the stream had gone over our soul. . . . Our help is in the name of the Lord, who made heaven and earth.'

"We prayed together our family prayer from Psalm 67, asking God's mercy and blessing—'That thy way may be known upon earth.' Then with cheerful voices we sang our morning hymn. I looked around me. The tears had stopped. There was firm ground under our feet again.

"It wasn't long until the reporters arrived. They wanted a picture of the family. I could see that this was confusing for the children. They always smile when a picture is going to be taken

—but now there was nothing to smile about.

"The reporter asked me why my husband had chosen to go at this time. I told him, 'He would never have gone if I had not urged him to do so. We both felt there was an important work to do in Africa. As for his family—we are provided for.'

"I went on about my morning work. From the kitchen window I could see Carl—he's just had his tenth birthday, you know—trudging up and down the maple lane. The sight made me wince with pain, for there was something about his little-boy figure, marching up and down so resolutely, his hands in his pockets, that reminded me of your father who walked just the same way when he was in the throes of a decision.

"A little later Carl came to me, his blue eyes serious with determination. 'Mother,' he announced, 'if it's true that Daddy was drowned, then I've decided to become a sailor when I grow up.'

"It was a little while afterward that your call came through."

The telephone conversation with Mother made me feel better. I would need the courage and strength which seemed such a contagious part of her being, for the long day still lay ahead of me—a day of hoping against hope.

I thought of Paul, my oldest brother, a freshman at the University of Missouri at Columbia. What kind of a day was he having? This in turn reminded me of the summer before when he had been our family chauffeur on a trip to Michigan. The summer in Michigan! It was really the last happy time when all of us were together as a family.

Late that spring we had heard from Father that he found a vacant cottage in his parish and the congregation was furnishing it for us. We could join him! Except for Paul, whose responsibility as chauffeur weighed heavily on him, we all looked forward to the exciting adventure. We weren't in the least dismayed at the prospect of squeezing eleven of us into a worn-out car and setting forth on a trip of a thousand miles.

The great moment arrived. The old 1926 Packard had been

greased, tires checked, seating plan worked out. Paul wrapped the cardboard boxes that contained our summer wardrobes in an old piece of canvas, which he tied securely on the right running board, fastening the ends of the rope to the door handles.

We took our places. Mother had to slip under the steering wheel to get to her seat on the front right side. Two-year-old David was lifted in through the open window and put on her lap. Veda, twelve, who had trouble keeping her long copper-colored braids out of the reach of her brothers, was to sit in the middle of the front seat. John and I, both in our early teens, would be in charge of the back-seat passengers—Mary, four, and Gustav, six. Carl, Martha, and Eunice, the middle trio in the age bracket, were perched precariously on folding chairs amidships.

Paul checked the oil once more, closed the engine hood, and took his place behind the steering wheel. All set? But no. Where was John?

He came running up with the road maps and his geography books, for he was to be the guide. As usual, his shirttail was out and his red hair tousled, but that didn't worry him. He put one foot up on the back fender and slipped adroitly through the open window into the back seat and we were ready to go. No need to shut the door as God did with Noah's ark—it was already closed.

Paul stepped on the starter. We were rewarded by the obedient and aristocratic purr of the Packard. We sang lustily as we rolled down the long maple-bordered lane of our driveway and headed northeast.

Every time we came to a stop light, people along the road would stare at us, then start counting heads. I myself was startled whenever I caught a glimpse of the car reflected in the store windows.

The long, square, classic lines of the engine hood would have given an air of quiet dignity to the old-fashioned black car—except for all the heads. Most of them were blonds, but there were four redheads, too. And the way the baggage carrier bulged with the cardboard boxes on the running board! Real hillbillies—

that's what they'd say when they saw us coming in Michigan. Being at that stage of adolescence where I was much concerned about the opinions of others, I said to John:

"What do you suppose people think of us?"

He gave a shrug and a typical John-answer:

"I'm sure I don't care."

Two days later Paul brought our faithful bus to a quiet stop in front of what would be our summer home.

A tall familiar figure threw open the front door. Yes, it was our father. He came down the steps to the car, his face radiant. We knew it was no use rushing to him until Mother had the first kiss. Then it would be our turn, each one, to hear his word of exclamation or praise as we were enfolded in his arms.

We turned to look at the house.

A big welcome sign was on the door. Inside, in the mellow glow of a kerosene lamp, we spied a long wooden table set for twelve, loaded down with food enough for twenty.

We rushed to explore the house. In each room we found new surprises. An old grand piano in the living room caught our fancy. It was hopelessly out of tune, but elegant nevertheless.

After supper, as we joined hands to form our family circle, John remarked:

"Do you know, this will be the first night in our lives that all twelve of us have slept under one roof?"

And so it was, for our three-room stone cottage in the Ozarks had long ago become too small. We had had to convert a chicken house into the girls' dorm and the old smoke house into the dorm for the boys.

It had been such a wonderful summer in Stonington with the quiet waves of Lake Michigan lapping at the landing pier just a hundred feet in front of our house. We had spent it—all twelve of us—playing, working, fishing, swimming, singing together, having a happy time.

Where was Father now? Was he really lost at sea? I still could not believe it. The latest broadcast had brought us a thin ray of hope. It suggested that if any passengers had survived, there was a chance they might have been taken aboard a prison ship. Could this be true? If so, was he among them? How much longer would we have to endure the suspense? That day—May 19, 1941—was the longest day I had ever lived through.

I did not expect to fall asleep that night with all that was coursing through my mind. But I must have done so. The next thing I knew the phone was ringing.

I picked up the receiver and heard the operator say:

"Long distance calling."

An unfamiliar voice came on:

"This is Dr. Swanson from mission headquarters in Minneapolis." I wondered why he was calling me. Then he said: "We've just received good news from the United Press! Your father is alive and safe. So are the Norbergs and all the other missionaries and passengers. Will you tell your grandmother and mother?"

It was no longer Black Monday, but Tuesday, the 20th. The sun was shining. Birds were singing in the maple trees.

The world went round and round. It was like Easter joy. I called Mother immediately.

"Yes, I know," she replied calmly. "Mr. Ingram, our neighbor, spent all night at his short-wave set. He brought me the good news early this morning. They're safe at a German-occupied port. Paul called, too. He'd been up all night at the radio station in Columbia. He was there when word came through."

More details trickled out each day in the newspapers and over the radio. But we weren't terribly excited. We knew that when Father came home, we'd be treated to a firsthand account.

It was a month later that we learned he had left Portugal on the S.S. *Excalibur* and would arrive in New York June 30.

Two.

Cobblestone Cottage

We began at once to make plans for Father's home-coming. Mother, Paul, and little David would go in the Packard to our grandparents' home near Moline, Illinois. There they would meet Father when he arrived from New York. Veda was already there. Meanwhile, John and I would be in charge of the Homestead for a week.

Hardly had the car disappeared down the maple lane when I called a family council. We were seven now—the three brothers, John, Carl, and Gus, myself and three younger sisters, Eunie, Marty, and Mary.

"What are we going to do to surprise Daddy?" I asked my brothers and sisters, who had taken their seats around the big rectangular dining-room table. "We have exactly a week in which to get ready."

A thoughtful silence reigned.

Eunie uttered a small sound.

"Have you forgotten? The day Daddy gets home will be his birthday—July 9!"

I *had* forgotten.

"And you know what other important day it is too?" John

asked eagerly. "It's their wedding anniversary."

I recalled now some of those past birthdays.

"John!" I exclaimed. "Remember Daddy's birthday that time during the Depression when there was no money to pay our loan on the Homestead and how sad he was? So we were going to do everything we could to cheer him up?

"We got together a whole box of presents that we hoped would make him so happy that all his sadness would be chased away. You pasted up a funny marionette to get him to laugh; I painted a decorated motto telling him not to worry. Veda and Eunie made handkerchiefs for him out of old sugar sacks, then embroidered them. And the little ones filled scrapbooks with flowers from the seed catalogue. We wrapped each present carefully, then put them all together in a big carton with his initials on it."

Now it was Carl's turn.

"Yes, I remember that day," he said, nodding. "We all got up real early and sneaked outside their bedroom window. I think the best surprise for them was when we woke them up with the song we had been secretly practicing."

"Another one I remember," I put in, "was that first year I was in the 4-H Club and learning to sew. I wanted to make him something. So I tackled a pair of pajamas. The material was navy blue with white polka-dots. I got along all right with the cutting and stitching, but in my hurry to finish, I sewed the buttons on crooked. One side of the jacket was inches longer than the other side—and no time to fix it. But Daddy was so pleased he never let me change those buttons. He said he liked his lopsided pajamas because they were a reminder of his daughter's love."

Now Marty added:

"But what could we do this year for a surprise?"

"I've got an idea," I said. "But you'd all have to help."

Gus leaned across the table.

"Tell us!"

"You know that box full of wallpaper and paint that Uncle Mart sent down from his store in Wahoo?" I unfolded my idea. I felt six pairs of doubting eyes upon me.

Could we really paint and wallpaper the living room ourselves?

Then Eunie said:

"But it's always been this way—you don't see the spots so bad
when all the French windows are open and all twelve of us are in
this room."

Carl suggested:

"We could hang up Daddy's big Africa map again now that it's
summer and we've moved out the heating stove. That would
cover the place on the wall where the woodbox stood."

Indeed it would. That map was six feet by nine and was hung
up only when we had company.

"I'll bet we could fix the house, though, if we tried hard!" John
said. Then he turned to Gus and Carl. "You kids would have to
take over the chores. Eunie, you'd be chief cook and bottle
washer. And you younger ones would have to do—well, whatever you can. Shall we take a vote on it?"

Motion passed: 7-0.

For the next five days John and I struggled to carry out my
inspiration. But it wasn't anywhere near so easy as we had
thought. John, who had agreed to paint the ceiling, was a comical
sight. Drops of white paint specked his tousled hair and the tip of
his nose while he struggled manfully on.

"Can't you work a little faster, John?" I asked as I watched
him critically. "We haven't got much time, you know."

That did it.

"Want to try it yourself?" he demanded.

I took the brush from his hands. After five minutes my arm
and neck ached; I had to give it back. Then I tackled the wall-
papering. But I soon found that the paper had a preference for
sticking to me. Every few minutes I had to call John to my
rescue.

Many times during the hectic week I stopped and asked myself
if it were really worth the effort. Nevertheless, we made it. By

Saturday evening every piece of furniture was back in place.

And what a transformation! Ceiling and woodwork were freshly painted, and the walls bright with the light-colored paper. The map of Africa was hung, and a big painting of the S.S. *Gripsholm* was back in its place over the reed organ. The old Packard could drive up the lane any time now.

We waited an hour—two hours. We ate our supper cold. At last I had to put the younger children to bed, but only after promising to wake them up the minute I heard the car.

The next thing I knew someone was shaking me. I forced open my eyes. It was Paul.

"We're here! We're here!" he cried. "We drove all night."

The morning sun was streaming in the window. I heard Father's voice and ran into his arms. We had surprised him and Mother, all right. Our parents' look of proud approval and exclamations of praise as they gazed about them were reward enough for all the hours of work.

I, too, hardly recognized our little house. The Japanese wall vase was filled with fresh flowers. The hand-woven white cloth Mother had brought home from Tanganyika when I was a baby covered the dining-room table. Behind the hand-carved African stools, just the right height for the little ones to sit on during our Sunday evening story hour, were freshly papered walls.

Happiness, like sunshine, flooded every corner of the room as we joined hands around the breakfast table and sang our Sunday hymn, translated from the Swedish:

> Day of God, so sweet and fair, Call us now to praise and prayer,
> Gift of God to mortals giv'n, Foretaste of the joy of heav'n.
> When the week of labor ends, And the peace of heav'n descends,
> O how sweet it is to meet At our holy Saviour's feet!
> Gracious Lord, we look to Thee For Thy blessing, rich and free;
> May Thy gospel's glorious sound Echo all the world around.

When evening came we gathered in the living room. For as long as I could remember, it had been a family tradition to place our chairs in a circle and then to have a program with each one taking part. Usually we chose a David Livingstone story to read together. Then, after some family singing with Mother at the little organ, John and Carl would play their violins.

But tonight would be different. Father was about to tell his story, and we could hardly wait. Without any preliminaries he said, in his clear, familiar voice:

"Carl, bring me the globe on my desk. I want to show you the route we were to follow."

We crowded around his chair.

"See, the *Zamzam* left here from New York," he began, "then went down the Atlantic coastline to Recife, Brazil. From there we were to set out for Capetown, then travel up the east coast of Africa just as Mother and I had done when you, Paul, were a little baby. The Norbergs and I and all the other missionaries bound for Tanganyika were to disembark here at Mombasa."

He handed the globe to Carl, who put it back in its place. David crawled up on Father's lap and snuggled there contentedly as the story continued:

"We knew beforehand that most of the *Zamzam's* passengers would be missionaries. The ship was of Egyptian registry, and the only one on which they could get passage to Africa. How strange that we as Christians should be going out on a Moslem vessel.

"Darkness was gathering that evening of March 20 as we glided down the Hudson River and past the Statue of Liberty. It was bitter cold out there on deck, but I couldn't go in just yet.

"This moment was historic. Your Aunt Ida was standing beside me. She looked up at me and said: 'Ralph, from the expression on your face, I think you must be the happiest man on board.' 'Yes,' I answered, 'I believe I am. I'm on my way back to Africa at last. If only Gertrude and my children were at my side, my fulfillment would be complete.'

"I stayed there on the deck until the last lights faded away. I prayed for each and every one of you and then I went down to my cabin to write to you. I knew the *Zamzam* would be taking on more cargo at Baltimore and we could send our last greetings from there.

"Did you read what Mr. Murphy wrote in *Life* magazine about the scene as the *Zamzam* pulled out of Baltimore? He told how Capt. William Smith, a ruddy-faced little Scot, looked down un-happily from the bridge to the deck below where one hundred and twenty missionaries were singing 'Jesus, Saviour, Pilot Me' while other passengers tried to drown them out with an impudent song of their own.

"The captain turned to his chief engineer and said: 'Mark my words, Mr. Burns, no good will come of this. It's bad luck for a ship to have so many Bible punchers and sky pilots aboard!'

"But we thought otherwise. We knew that for every missionary on the ship there were thousands in the home churches who were praying. Surely God would heed these prayers.

"Once we headed for Trinidad, it was like a pleasant vacation trip. We soon left the gray winter far behind and could shed our business suits. I didn't lose any time changing into khaki, for that's the clothing in which I've always felt most comfortable."

"That's the way we like you best too, Daddy," Veda inter-rupted. "I'm glad you don't wear those round preacher collars all the time like some ministers do."

Father looked down at his clothes in surprise.

"You know, now that I stop to think of it," he said, "this is the same outfit I had on the morning the *Zamzam* was sunk."

"Even to the green necktie?" asked Marty.

"Yes, even to the necktie. But I'm getting ahead of my story. Wait a minute. Oh yes, I remember now what I was going to tell you. A lot of people began to come on deck in their sun helmets —all prepared for the tropics. But winter was behind us for sure the day the Catholic priests exchanged their black robes for trop-ical-weight white ones. We let out a big cheer when we saw them.

"A number of missionaries had their families along. Among them was Mrs. Danielson—you've probably read about her. She was traveling alone with her six children, on her way to rejoin her husband in Africa. I tell you she had her hands full keeping track of those youngsters.

"None of us will forget that Easter Sunday. First, there was a children's program in the lounge. Their happy Easter messages touched our hearts. Then, following the sermon, we had a communion service together. It was just what we needed. You know, this was the last Sunday before the big testing.

"Skies were sunny and the weather fair. But soon after we left Trinidad, we found out all was not well. Neutral ships have flags painted on their sides and run with lights. But here we were sneaking through the night in darkness.

"I remember groping my way to the cabin after an hour on deck under the stars. I'd knock carefully on the door. That was the signal for one of my cabin mates to turn out the light and cautiously open the door.

"We got our first scare Monday morning. Without any warning, the captain turned our ship sharply about and we raced back toward South America. For thirty hours our brave old vessel fled from death. Then we resumed our course to Capetown. We found out later that a ship just twenty miles away was being chased by a German raider.

"Mrs. Danielson told me that one of her daughters kept coming to her and saying: 'Mother, I'm scared the boat will sink. I just *know* it will!' Her mother tried to calm her, saying: 'We're riding safely. Jesus is our Pilot! Let's trust ourselves to Him.'

"I had no fear in my heart—only great joy that I was returning to Africa. I remember that beautiful sunset on the evening of April 16. I looked into it and thought of you. But my loneliness was so great that I went up to the Norberg family's cabin. Your aunt, uncle, and cousins were having their evening devotions. I had no idea that this was the last night of our ship's life.

"The next morning—it must have been before dawn—I was awakened by a loud *Bang!* At first I thought it was only a big wave that had slapped against the ship. No use trying to look out the porthole—it was painted over because of the blackouts. No, it wouldn't be a wave. The ship seemed steady, the sea calm. I got up from my bunk.

"*Wham—Bang!* Again it came.

"Overhead and all around me I heard things crashing and falling. Then I realized the terrible truth. The *Zamzam* was being shelled.

"One of my cabin mates rushed in. His face was deathly pale. 'A German raider is shooting at us!' he gasped. At that moment it came again. *Wham—Bang!*"

"Ooh!" Eunie cried out.

"Our cabin light went out," Father continued. "Everything was deathly still. Now the silence was even worse—after all that noise. It would be awful, I thought, to go down in darkness!

"I dressed—yes, I even put on this tie I'm wearing today, and the jacket. I slipped the strap of my binoculars case over my shoulder. Those glasses were your farewell present.

"I slipped my passport and the little leather folder with your pictures in it into my pocket. I started for the deck. Suddenly I remembered I did not have my watch. It was one that my father had given me when I was a boy. I ran back to my cabin and got it. But in my hurry, I forgot my wallet with my money in it.

"When I came to the foot of the gangway leading to the upper deck, I saw how serious the situation was. Two of our neighbors were lying there badly wounded. I stopped to see if I could help, but they were already being treated by one of the missionary doctors. The long, narrow corridor was jammed with frightened, shouting passengers. The ship was already listing.

"I didn't breathe freely until I reached the open space on our deck. There I got my first glimpse of the raider. Murphy described her well in *Life* when he said: 'If ever a ship looked the role, she did—a ship of ambush, very low in the water, black against the dawn.' She had stopped firing when I saw her, and was flashing signal lights.

"It was all I could do to climb up the steep, narrow gangway to our lifeboat station, because so many were trying to do it at the same time. But I made it just as the lifeboat was being lowered from the boat deck above. Then I let out a cry: 'Thank God, there's Mrs. Danielson!' We helped the children into the lifeboats. They couldn't have been more brave. There was much confusion among the Egyptian sailors as we were lowered into the water.

"Down we went, smoothly enough until we almost touched the sea. Just then the rope slipped off the pole! It flew back and hit Mrs. Danielson on the crown of the head. Fortunately, it didn't knock her unconscious.

"That poor mother—as if she wasn't having enough trouble. Her foot was bleeding. It had been cut by broken glass in her cabin. As the lifeboat rocked on the swells, she told me of the nightmare of those first minutes in their crowded cabin.

"A shell had hit right above them. Glasses, pitchers, and mirror came crashing to the deck, which was slanting so, they could hardly stand up. The lights went out. In the dark they heard the whine of other shells, and wondered which would strike next. Everywhere were nerve-racking noises: the frantic crying of her littlest ones, the awed whispers of the older children, the moaning of wounded passengers in the halls. She prayed steadily, while getting life belts on the youngsters: 'Lord, save us, but Thy will be done. Be gracious to our Daddy if this is our last morning.' Then they all joined hands and rushed out the cabin door and down to their lifeboat station.

"Suddenly, as Mrs. Danielson was telling me her story, the words died on her lips. She was pointing to the bottom of the boat. I saw with great consternation that we were taking water. Everyone grabbed a can or a bucket and started to bail. But in a few minutes the water was up to our knees. We saw now that we couldn't bail fast enough to keep afloat, but we kept at it anyway. Meanwhile, the Egyptian sailors pulled frantically at the oars, trying to get our lifeboat clear of the stern of the sinking *Zamzam* before the ship went down and took us with it.

"In the excitement several of the passengers must have shifted positions. Suddenly the lifeboat turned over, throwing the occupants into the sea.

"Since I had been one of the last to board the boat, I was near the rudder and could slide into the water. I was kept up by my life jacket. An oar floated within my reach and I grabbed it. With great relief I noticed that we had passed the stern of the *Zamzam*. Then I realized that we were drifting out into the vast open spaces of the Atlantic.

"But the Danielson children—where were they? At that moment I saw them. Lawrence, the oldest, was kicking and pushing a sailor who had fallen right on top of his little sister when the boat capsized. He managed to pull her to the edge of the overturned boat so she could hang on.

"A little farther away, I saw Mrs. Danielson. She was struggling desperately. Wilfred, her three-year-old, had a life preserver. But it was far too heavy for him and kept pulling his head backward into the water. She kept a firm grip on him. Then I saw that the brave mother was also holding her youngest, Lois, who had no life jacket, in the crook of her left arm. My soul cried out to Almighty God. I couldn't get near enough to help them. The little ones whimpered. Mrs. Danielson said to them: 'Don't try to pray out loud. Keep your mouths closed because of the salty water. Pray in your hearts. Jesus loves you even more than Daddy and Mother.'

"We missionaries also prayed silently for cleansing—that if this were our last hour, we might be ready to meet our God.

"One of the sailors had scrambled up onto the bottom of the overturned lifeboat and was imploring his Allah for help. I called out to him: 'The best way you can serve Allah is to pull those two little children up there on the boat with you.' He did so, and before long, little Wilfred and his sister Luella were lying on their tummies on the upturned boat.

"Oh, the pitiful sight of those two blue and shivering youngsters with their teeth chattering in that chilly dawn.

"Now I had to turn my attention to Mrs. Danielson. I slipped my oar under her right arm, for I could see that she was losing strength rapidly. I could only ask myself: 'God, how long?'

"For a moment I was comforted to think that the water was not cold. Then a shudder ran through me, for it meant the sea could be shark-infested. Those who, like Mrs. Danielson, had received cuts and wounds would be in special danger, for I'd read that fresh blood attracts sharks.

"The sun was rising. It gave me my bearings; over there must be the east. In that direction lay the continent of Africa. Only a few more days, if all had gone well, and we would have landed there. But now—this.

"I looked in the direction of the raider. She was slowly moving toward us. She drew nearer and nearer until we found ourselves right at her side. We bobbed along toward the stern.

"Now we were in danger of being caught in the propellers. We signaled frantically to the men along the rail to come to our aid before it was too late. One of the men in the water called out to us: 'It's no use—they're not going to help a feller after they've done this!'

"We took heart when we saw two launches being lowered off the raider's upper deck. One set out to go to the aid of another lifeboat which was in trouble, having almost capsized. The other went around picking survivors out of the water, one by one.

"Strong arms pulled the little children up into the German boat. The rest of us—men and women both—clambered aboard. This was hard because our wet clothing was a drag on us.

"*Chug! Chug!* we were on our way to the raider. We stopped right below the big rope ladder dangling over its side. Mrs. Danielson went up first, followed by her older children. Lois and Wilfred remained in the launch. A German sailor was staring down at us. My first thought was that when I reached the deck of the raider, he was going to shove me right back into the water. Instead, he threw a blanket around my shoulders and gave me a cup of hot tea.

"A ship's officer helped Mrs. Danielson and the older children get off their dripping life jackets. He said to her: 'Follow me into a warm room.'

"She replied, 'I can't until all my children are safe.'

"He looked at the four children clustered around her and gasped: '*Mein Gott!* One, two, three, four! Are there more?'

"Just then a straw basket was hoisted over the railing and plumped down at our feet. I could see the outstretched arms and big brown eyes of little Lois Danielson.

"Another basket came over the edge. In it sat Wilfred, drenched, shivering, and blue. But a smile spread slowly over his face when he saw that he was safe, high up above the water.

"The shivering survivors were all on deck now. A count was made. No life had been lost, although three passengers were badly wounded and were being cared for by the ship's surgeon. The children were without a scratch. There were no serious injuries among the missionaries.

"Suddenly I noticed the passengers were gazing excitedly at the sky. I looked up and saw a perfect rainbow of unusual brilliance. The covenant of God's love to His people—rainbow dawn—I thought. None of us who saw it would ever forget it.

"God had helped us thus far. He still would lead us."

"And what happened to Aunt Ida and Uncle Einar?" Carl asked.

"Oh, I quite forgot to tell you about them," Father said. "I'm sorry. They were in another lifeboat, you see. I was greatly relieved when I noticed them safely on board the rescue ship. And do you know, they didn't even get wet!"

Father paused again and then went on.

"So there I was on deck, trying to dry my clothes. And even more important to me—trying to salvage your pictures, which were almost ruined by the salt water.

"We watched the launches making trip after trip to the *Zamzam*, bringing loose clothing, suitcases, trunks, typewriters, food, cigarettes, soap, and other goods. About two-thirty in the afternoon the last one pulled away.

"A few minutes later a deep, heavy boom announced that the first time bomb the German sailors had planted in the *Zamzam* had exploded. Speechless with emotion, we watched the ship slowly settle to her grave. A second blast, then a third, sent columns of water up through the hatches and the funnels. At last she rolled over and slipped beneath the waters, leaving only scattered wreckage and debris to mark the spot.

"It was a bitter moment. All the hospital equipment your Uncle Einar and Aunt Ida had bought for their medical work in Tanganyika was at the bottom of the ocean. On board had been twenty ambulances for the British-American Ambulance Corps.

"One man had a twenty-five-hundred-dollar stamp collection in his trunks. A German officer, interested in stamp collecting, actually shed tears when he heard this later.

"We chose a committee of five to represent the passengers before the captain of the raider. Pastor Johnson, spokesman for the missionaries, gave us a good report when he came back. He described Captain Rogge as a large athletic man, about forty-five, with a genial personality. Speaking through an interpreter, Captain Rogge apologized for having shelled the *Zamzam*. He justified his action by saying that the *Zamzam* was traveling completely blacked out, not even showing navigation lights.

"Next day we were transferred to a German freighter, the *Dresden*. The ship had accommodations for thirty-five passengers; but now she carried many times that number—eighty-seven of them women and children.

"We were in the South Atlantic, about midway between South America and Africa. In whatever direction we might go, we would be in danger. I thought of Jonah and how he must have felt when he cried out to God and said: 'Thou didst cast me into the depth, in the heart of the seas, and the flood was round about me' [2:3].

"We came up the gangway of the *Dresden*. Women and children were sent to the upper deck amidships. The Number Two hatch was open. A stairway, newly constructed, led into the hold.

We were ordered by the German officers to go below. Reluctantly we obeyed—ninety-one male passengers and the nineteen officers of the *Zamzam*.

"We found ourselves a bewildered and forlorn lot, in a bare room just a little more than fifty feet square. The heavy steel plate of the main deck was our ceiling. There were no portholes, no ventilation except the hatch. Stories of the misery of African slaves brought to America 'under hatches' a hundred years ago came flooding to my mind. Compared to them, we were well off.

"Gradually our eyes became accustomed to the semidarkness. We soon discovered that there was not a stick of furniture, not even a bench, only several bales of cotton stacked against a bulkhead.

"Presently a guard brought us an armful of narrow, unbleached muslin bags, which he passed out to us, saying we could fill them from the bales. This was a tedious business because the pressed cotton had to be carefully fluffed out. All the bags were the same length—not quite long enough for us six-footers, so we had to use our life preservers as an extension. But at least it gave us a certain sense of security to know that they would be near at hand if we had to make a hurried exit from the ship.

"Along toward six o'clock, the Egyptian stewards came down into the hold with dishpans of soup. Each one of us was handed an enamel bowl, an aluminum cup, and a spoon. They ladled out the soup to us. Then we were each given two pieces of brown bread and a cup of tea. Later we were allowed to go on deck to wash our utensils at a hydrant drawing ocean water. How good it was to get out of the stuffy hold and breathe fresh air!

"But fifteen minutes after sunset the guards ordered all of us below. Two rather dim lights had been placed in the far corners. The glow disclosed a strange spectacle: Over a hundred men of all ages were strung out, covering most of the floor space.

"After an hour or so of chatting, and the singing of one or two songs, all became quiet. It had been another day of stress and strain. Yet, when I closed my eyes that first night, it was as though the Prince of Peace Himself was walking the waters, saying to us: 'Be not afraid. . . . It is I. . . . I am with you.'

"Fifteen minutes before sunrise the guard called: 'All out.' We obeyed gladly after the long weary hours in close quarters. We were doled out about three cupfuls of water. our daily ration for washing and shaving. Then came breakfast, consisting of a bowl of slightly sweetened starchy gruel—the men called it 'billboard paste'—and a couple of slices of brown bread with tea.

"That morning Captain Jaeger of the *Dresden* paid us a visit. He told us that he didn't know how long we would have to remain on the ship, but he thought that we should count on at least a month. We all groaned inwardly. A month! All lifeboats and rafts were being overhauled. We grasped the significance: At any hour of the day or night we might find it necessary to leave the ship on short notice.

"For about nine days the *Dresden* idled and rolled, going nowhere in the South Atlantic. We were right on the Equator. The iron deck above us, baking in the tropical sun, was like a stove. Men who had neither shoes nor hats suffered acutely. The stuffiness and heat of the nights were almost unbearable. By this time many had become ill with dysentery.

"I couldn't sleep much those long nights in the hold. Once I even said to Uncle Einar: 'It wouldn't be so bad if only Gertrude and the children were here.' He retorted: 'Just be glad they're not.'

"Of course, he was right. Soldiers cannot take their families to the battlefield. Then, somehow, knowing that you were back at the Homestead in the Ozarks made me stronger.

"I knew that at home it would be springtime. Everywhere it would be green—that color which nourishes the soul. Perhaps the apricot trees were already in bloom. I could just see the new leaves on the Chinese elms that I'd planted to celebrate your birth dates . . . The light jade green of the Russian olive tree I'd planted the day Gus was born . . . Eunie's Rose of Sharon . . . It was the time when everything was being born anew.

"What a world apart from what I was experiencing in the sweltering heat below hatch Number Two . . . where Catholic priests, tobacco buyers, scientists, older missionaries, first termers, and ambulance drivers were all crowded elbow to elbow.

"Now we entered the most dangerous part of our trip; we were to run the British blockade. We feared the submarines most. A torpedo amidships would finish us off. We finally persuaded Captain Jaeger to give us rope and wood to make two ladders leading out of the hatch. We worked out our own 'abandon ship' routine. After a few drills we proved we could clear the hatch in about sixty-five seconds.

"We slept fully dressed, with our life jackets always near at hand. By now we were in the area of the Atlantic where it was cold, so we needed all the clothes we could lay hands on. We began each night knowing that it might very well be our last."

John interrupted here.

"But, Daddy, when all these things happened to you, I should think you'd be sad. But you're not."

"You're right, John." Father leaned forward in his chair. "Something happened to all of us on that prison ship. Passages in God's Word we hadn't noticed before took on a new meaning. And, too, when you face death daily as we did, children, you ask yourself only one question: 'Do I have peace with God?' And if you do, then nothing else matters very much."

Father looked around the circle and went on:

"Twice a week, which was all I was allowed, I used to visit with Aunt Ida and her family. Then I'd go and tap at the window of Mrs. Danielson's cabin. I told her how we in the hold often prayed for her and especially for her husband the day that he heard the news in Africa of the *Zamzam's* sinking. She in turn reassured me that many of the women were praying for you, Gertrude, and for the children.

"We hadn't been on our eastward course very long before we ran into stormy weather. A biting cold wind arose, bringing with it the rain and the mist, narrowing down our little world. We were worried when we saw the rising waves. We hoped we would not have to take to the lifeboats in such a heaving sea.

"Only later did we learn that the very conditions which bothered us so much had made it impossible for submarines and airplanes to operate against us. So even here God was giving us His protection.

"Shortly after sunset on Sunday, May 18, we noticed a faint flicker along the horizon. Could it possibly be a lighthouse? Our eager voices reached the captain on the bridge. He called down to us: 'What's all the excitement about down there? Didn't I tell you we would see land within twenty-four hours?'

"And land it was.

"A businessman among us said then: 'Captain Jaeger may attribute his bringing us safely to port to his luck if he pleases. But as for myself, I am convinced that God answered the prayers of the missionaries.' Many voices were lifted in thanksgiving and praise from the prison ship that night.

"On the morning of May 20 we anchored safely in the French harbor of Saint-Jean-de-Luz.

"My passport was returned to me by the purser. When I started to go away, he called me back to hand me my wallet. One of the sailors had found it under my pillow on the *Zamzam* on the morning of the shelling. I was both amazed and happy.

"We went ashore for a few minutes along the quai.

"And do you know what was the first thing I bought once my feet were on solid ground? I picked out a bunch of carrots from a little vegetable stand, and ate them just as they were, tops and all. Nothing could have tasted better after having been starved of vitamins for so long.

"Ten days later, representatives of the U.S. Embassy from Madrid escorted us to Spain. At last we were on neutral soil. Now we could turn our eyes toward the freedom and joy of our homeland."

No one said anything as Father finished his story. But one big question was uppermost in our minds. What would he do now? It was a question that nobody dared put into words.

We did not see much of Father during the next few months. He spent his time telling church groups throughout the Midwest about his experiences on the *Zamzam*. Sometimes he sent us the newspaper clippings. Typical was this one:

" . . . Tall, quiet, unassuming, Rev. Ralph Hult's simple recital of the facts concerning the sinking of the Egyptian ship, *Zamzam*, provided his audience with a first-hand chapter out of world history. He spoke without rancor toward his German captors or the chain of circumstances which led to his experience. . . ."

But this kind of witness could not satisfy him for long. He had to get back to Africa. Urgent calls for his help continued to come from Tanganyika. The need for experienced missionaries was acute.

Early on a May morning, ten months after our happy reunion, we went with Father to the railroad station in Springfield to say good-by. He was on his way to New York to find a ship that would take him again to Africa.

In the last busy days of packing, I had typed for him a letter to his sister Ida which summed up his reasons for trying once more:

"I can have no peace of mind until we have exhausted every possible means of going out to the field. My family is absolutely at one with me in the desire and hope that I may get out to Africa at this time, just as they were a year ago before the sinking. As soldiers of the Cross' we should not retreat until the war clouds clear away, but rather go forward. May God be merciful unto us. . . . 'That thy way may be known upon earth, thy salvation among all nations.' "

The train that would take Father away was filled with soldiers. They were wearing khaki as he was. The dreadful news of Pearl Harbor in December had plunged our nation into war.

Mother's eyes were clear as she bade him farewell. She would cry, but not until later, behind a closed door. Now her face was transfigured with a rare beauty, a beauty born of courage, unselfishness, and greatness of heart.

The engine tooted, wheezed, and puffed. The wheels began to turn. The train was pulling out. Father waved to us from the window.

"There he goes, children," Mother said, "the bravest and truest soldier of them all." And she waved and waved until the crowd had melted away and the train was only a speck in the distance.

Three.

Tularemia

John's face was white as he came hurrying up the steps to the Kollmeyer house in Springfield one morning, three weeks after Father had left. I had seen the Packard arrive as I was clearing away the breakfast dishes.

"Ingrid! You've got to come home right away!"

"What is it?"

"Mother's sick, sicker than I've ever seen her."

Mrs. Kollmeyer couldn't help overhearing. She was due to go to the hospital for her third baby any day now, so I was helping her for the summer.

"You must go with him right away," she said without hesitation. "I can handle the rest of your work all right."

Once we were by ourselves in the car, John gave me the whole story.

"Well," he began, "three days ago she began to be feverish. She called Dr. Knabb and he ordered some of those new sulfa drugs for her. I went into town to pick them up. But I met one of my high school friends in the drugstore, got started talking and almost forgot the medicine. It was nearly dark by the time I got home. I found Mother in tears.

" 'John, John, where have you been?' she said. 'I was so worried. Did anything break down on the car?'

"You know I was so ashamed then, Ingrid. I told her how I'd got started talking to Jim and forgot all about time. She said, 'Don't you know, John, now that your father's gone and Paul is working away from home, that you're the man of the house? I've got to be able to depend on you.' "

"But why didn't you call me right away?"

"She didn't want you to leave Mrs. Kollmeyer. Anyway, she thought she'd be better. But now the prescription is all used up and her fever is higher than ever. Sometimes I can hardly understand what she's trying to say."

By the time we reached home, I was terribly worried.

I hurried into the stone cottage which had been home almost as long as I could remember, and into Mother's bedroom.

Always so strong and cheerful, Mother now lay there helpless. I noticed that her brown hair was already quite gray around the temples. Her face brightened when she saw me, but she could speak only with difficulty. Then I saw a nasty swelling. John said it seemed to come from the gland under her armpit where a wood tick had bitten her several days before. Could this, I wondered, be the cause of her strange illness?

I called Dr. Knabb, who came right away. He took one look and said we had to get Mother to the hospital. He phoned at once for an ambulance.

Mother tried to smile as she was being carried out the front door.

"It's all right, children," she said. "I'll be back home in three days. You know how to carry on until then. Be sure you finish the letter I started to Daddy—but don't tell him I'm sick. We don't want him to worry."

There we stood—nine children, David, the youngest, just four, and John, the oldest, not quite eighteen—watching the long black car drive out the lane and turn toward Springfield. We knew only too well it served as a hearse as well as an ambulance.

We had only recently said good-by to our father, not knowing whether we would ever see him again. Now Mother was leaving us, too. We looked bleakly at one another.

John picked up David and gave him a squeeze.

"Come back into the house, all of you," he said cheerily. "Let's make a family circle. I want to tell you a story."

Good old John! Already he was taking seriously his role as "man of the family." We didn't mind being bossed by him. Everybody loved him, and we, his sisters and brothers, most of all. He'd had to suffer for that bright red hair, especially the first years in grade school when the older boys teased him. But the total combination of mischievous blue eyes, freckled nose, and friendly grin were enough to soften the stoniest heart.

John was always getting sidetracked. How like him to forget the medicine, then feel remorseful about it! If he was supposed to water the cows, he'd likely be found watching an anthill under an apple tree. He could be so absorbed in studying spiders—he kept a collection of live tarantulas in an old cookie box—or frogs, that many a time he didn't hear Mother when she called: "Dinner's ready!"

Now we pulled up our chairs and sat down. Through the open window we could hear the mockingbird in the hickory tree.

"I know how you must feel," John said, looking around at our wan faces. "We've never seen Mother sick before, unless you count those times when we got a new brother or sister. But that always happened right here. She never left us, so we weren't frightened."

"John," Carl reminded him, "you said you'd tell us a story. Why don't you tell about when each of us was born?"

We clapped our hands in anticipation.

"I can remember very well, Carl, the day *you* were born," John said with a grin. "We had only moved here three months before, in October, 1930. We didn't have any boys' cottage or girls' cottage then as we do now. Paul, Ingrid, Veda, and I slept right here in the living room, crosswise on a double bed. Eunie was not yet two, so she still had the crib.

"Daddy had to call the doctor in the middle of the night. His name was Dr. Hogg, which made us laugh. He was big and jolly and tickled our toes when he saw us all lying there with our feet sticking out. Then he told us we had to behave because our new brother or sister would be along any minute. Aunt Bessie Clark had come with Dr. Hogg. She had on a nurse's uniform and was hurrying back and forth from the kitchen to the bedroom.

"I was worried, because I could hear through the door to the bedroom that Mother was suffering. Then there was a cry. That got us excited. A minute later Daddy came out of the bedroom with a baby in his arms.

" 'Here's your new brother,' he said, and introduced you to each one of us. We got to watch while Aunt Bessie weighed you—almost ten pounds you were—and while she gave you your first bath there on the dining-room table. You were so mad, you kicked the powder can right off onto the floor."

I put in:

"Before Dr. Hogg left, I remember he told Daddy and Mother that they had enough children now."

"Well, I'm glad they didn't agree with him," Veda said. "Just think! What if we didn't have any Marty, or Gus, or Mary, or David?"

John took up the story again.

"Did you know you were paid for with eggs, Carl?"

Carl shook his head.

"For a long time after you came, every Saturday when Daddy went to town, he took eggs to the doctor's house until the bill was paid. I remember, too, when we gave you a name. We liked Carl—Daddy explained that that means 'man' in Swedish—and to go with it he picked Eugene, which means 'well-born.' Carl Eugene—well-born man."

John turned to Marty.

"And then by the time you were born, two years later," he continued, "we had decided to call our home here Bethany, because that's where Jesus loved to visit Mary and Martha and their brother. So naturally we had to name you Martha. Did you know your middle name, Irene, means 'peace'?"

"Oh yes," I interrupted. "And we called Marty our 'Depression Baby.' "

"What does *that* mean?" Gus asked.

"It was a time when we hardly had any money," John explained. "Daddy wasn't preaching anywhere. We had to live on what we could raise on the land. Our parents told us that with the milk and eggs and all our fruit trees, besides the big vegetable garden, we weren't nearly as bad off as a lot of city families. Besides, we could sell our extra eggs and cream and use the money to buy a few groceries."

John turned to Gus.

"You have a king's name, Gus. Did you know that?" Gus looked impressed. "When you were born in 1934 we named you after King Gustaf of Sweden and also after Mother's father, Gustav Julius.

"It wasn't hard to find a name for you, Mary. Since we already had a Martha, you had to be Mary. But what did stump us was the middle name. We thought and thought. Then one day at dinnertime Veda announced, clapping her hands: 'I know it! I know it! Mary's middle name should be Leona, like Mother's.' We all agreed."

I broke in then with something that John hadn't mentioned.

"When *you* were born, Gus, that made us even: four blonds and four redheads; four boys and four girls. With Mary's coming we were five girls and five blonds. So we were convinced that Number Ten would be another brother and another redhead to even things up."

"That's right," John said. "And in April, 1938, *you* arrived, David—our twelve-pound brother. But we had to give up on the red hair. You put the blonds ahead six to four. The doctor said you were the biggest baby he ever delivered, but we thought you were the nicest. Eunie said you should be named Lazarus, since we had a Mary and a Martha. But the rest of us voted for David. I suppose we'd read so many stories about David Livingstone that he seemed like one of the family.

"And your second name, Ansgar, was the name of a missionary, and a famous one, too. Ansgar was a Frenchman, the first missionary from the Christian world to the Swedes. See, right here's a picture of him when he first arrived in Sweden centuries ago. Daddy framed it for us and hung it over the bookcase. David Ansgar Hult—that's quite a name to live up to, little brother," John concluded. David sat with his shoulders hunched, as though feeling the weight of his name.

But I wanted to add to David's story.

"I'll never forget the letter Mother received when David was only a few days old," I said. "Someone had written her, saying: 'Well, Gertrude, I don't know whether to feel sorry for you or not—having another child.'

"I was really taken aback when I read that. *Sorry* for her? When we had a new baby brother? I thought we were just about the luckiest family in the world."

Everybody laughed. But the laughter was followed by a sudden silence. We all knew we had come to the end of our diversion. Unpleasant reality was crowding in on us again.

John looked around the circle as though reading our thoughts.

"We'll try to go ahead with our work as if Daddy and Mother were here," he said with firmness and spirit. "That's what they'd want us to do. Now let's sing 'Children of the Heavenly Father.' "

John gave us the pitch, and we joined in. We felt better afterward. The last verse especially comforted us:

> Though He giveth or He taketh,
> God His children ne'er forsaketh.
> His the loving purpose solely,
> To preserve them pure and holy.

"Carl and I will be in charge of work on the farm," John said, continuing in his reassuring businesslike tone. "Besides that, Carl has his job at the neighbors milking their cows morning and night. I'll take care of marketing the cream and eggs, for that's the only cash money we're going to have this month."

He turned to me:

"Ingrid, you'll have to go back to the Kollmeyers. They're counting on you." I protested. "Besides, if you're in town," he urged, "then you can go every evening to visit Mother in the hospital." He looked over toward the others. "Veda, Eunie, Marty, you'll do the cooking, canning, washing, and ironing. And you three younger ones," he said, looking at Gus, Mary, and little David, who were waiting expectantly, "you're all good weed pullers. You can help with the garden. You can pick up the apples, too. If you help real well, I'll take you fishing."

"Can we go this afternoon?" Gus asked eagerly.

"Not this afternoon," John replied. "We promised Mother we'd finish the letter she started to Daddy, so he'll be sure to have it when he arrives in Capetown."

John went to get some writing paper and an envelope from Father's desk. Suddenly he cried:

"Look! Here's his last letter from New York, postmarked June 9. I think I'll read it to you now."

John began in a steady voice:

Thank you for all the encouraging messages you have sent me. It is remarkable that anyone gets the chance to go to Africa who is not connected with war service. We are happy that our government recognizes that foreign missionaries are rendering a distinct service in times like these. May we prove worthy of the confidence placed in us.

Ingrid, I won't forget the little message you wrote to me. You quoted the words of the devotional we read that last morning together: "To go out on thin ice (or dangerous waters) would be to tempt God, but to cross the ice (or ocean) if duty called us to do so would be to trust God."

The mail will be picked up very soon, so I must conclude this visit. I love you each one, my dear children, more than words can say. Be brave and strong. Help your mother, and go to her with all your problems. Pray for "journeying mercies" for me.

Love,
Daddy

The sunlight was streaming in through the open window. We sat down around the dining-room table to answer the letter. John gave us each a sheet of paper. But all we could think of was that Mother was sick and we couldn't mention it. The little ones chewed the ends of their pencils and looked at one another blankly.

Finally Carl broke the block. He said he was going to tell about the eggs he had sold from his own hens, and also how he would pay from his own money the postage for this airmail letter to Africa, which then cost well over a dollar. John said he was going to tell about the car, that it was running fine except for some axle trouble. Veda mentioned the trees which she knew were so dear to Father's heart. "All the evergreens you planted are doing nicely," she read aloud. "For a while we thought the Platte River Juniper was not going to live. But it's better now." (Veda was proud of the fact that she was the only child born in the same state as Father.)

At last we were started.

Gus, who'd just finished second grade, wrote with a sprawling hand: "I am fine except for my big toe. I stubbed it. I'm going to help John a lot this summer. I can ride the bicycle."

Poor Gus. He was never without a bruised finger, a scratched knee, or a stubbed toe.

Mary dictated her letter to me. She told about losing her first tooth; also that Blackie had some kittens. I wrote it down. Pretty soon she would start school and then she could write to her Daddy all by herself.

I had never been inside Burge Hospital before. It was an oppressively large brick building on busy Jefferson Street in Springfield. I found Mother's bed in the crowded women's ward. She gave me a smile of recognition, but it was a great effort for her to talk. She wanted to know how John and the children were getting along. I combed her hair, which seemed to soothe her. I had been there only a few minutes when the nurse said I must leave.

On Wednesday Dr. Knabb told me her condition was very serious. Her temperature soared to one hundred five degrees, sometimes going even higher. Her case had been diagnosed as a typhoid type of tularemia, caused by a wood-tick bite. Not even the sulfa seemed to help her. All that could be done for her was to see that she got good hospital care. I felt stricken inside.

Every evening as soon as I could leave my work, I hurried to the hospital. One night when she greeted me, Mother's eyes were shining.

"Do you know the wonderful thing that happened to me today?" she said as I sat down beside her. And then she related this incident:

"I've told you that Daddy is always so near to me in these days. At least his spiritual presence is near. But today he was actually here. I could feel him holding my hand and stroking my forehead.

"He came by plane—a special mail plane from South America. His ship was to be in port at Recife, Brazil, for two or three days. When he heard that a plane would be going from there straight to Springfield, he took it. It was worth it, he said, even though he could stay only a little while. It was so wonderfully comforting to have him here, talking to me, understanding this valley I'm going through.

"I told him how well you children were carrying on. He was so proud of you. Then his time was up. He had some kind of a prearranged signal, so he knew when he had to leave to join his plane again. I so much wanted you to see him before he left— that's why I kept calling for you. Oh, Ingrid, how good God was to me, to arrange his visit even for this short time!"

I couldn't say a word. It all seemed so logical as she spoke. But it couldn't be true. Was her illness affecting her mind? The world seemed very dark that evening as I walked home.

The next night she was so delirious she scarcely recognized me. I was terribly frightened. Where could I go for help? I thought of Pastor Koerber who lived only a few blocks from the hospital. I walked quickly to his house.

Pastor Koerber's face was very grave as he paced up and down the floor of his study.

"Yes, I know, Ingrid," he said, looking at me directly, "your mother is a very sick woman. Her life hangs in the balance. I must tell you that your father, too, is in great danger. So many vessels are being sunk off the Atlantic Coast. And he had to leave in a secret convoy, so we don't even know the name of his ship. I think you know what that means. As I told John this afternoon when he stopped by, you children will have to prepare yourselves to lose both your parents."

I stared at him in disbelief. I couldn't imagine such a thing. Yet that was what he was saying. Now I realized that I'd been so occupied that I never really faced up to the possibility. Stunned, I sat down abruptly.

He put his hand on my shoulder, this kind pastor whom I respected deeply.

"You are the oldest daughter in the family, Ingrid. I must be frank with you," he said. "You must prepare yourself. Your parents have always taught you to be strong, to think independently, to take responsibility. Here is your opportunity to live up to what they've taught you—to be worthy of them. Everyone who sends a soldier out to a battlefield has to expect this. It's no time for self-pity."

I thought of his words as I walked home that June night. I was glad of the distance, which was more than four miles. I needed time to reflect.

My route lay through the residential district, under the wide elm trees. Here I charted my way from one street lamp to the next—from light into darkness, from darkness into light.

It's true, I thought, this is the worst day I can ever remember, worse than the day we heard about the *Zamzam*. But if I just keep on walking straight ahead, I will come again into light. I can't stand here in this dark place. I have to walk to that next pool of light under the lamp post. Then the next and the next. And so I will reach my goal.

Strangely enough, by the time I got home I was no longer panicky. I was learning a basic lesson: that seeing things as they are, no matter how unpleasant they may be, and facing reality soberly, does not weaken us, but makes us stronger. When I opened the door, I could almost rejoice. I knew that whatever might happen, God would help us.

John called Uncle Lenus, Father's youngest brother, who lived in Oklahoma City. He promised to come right away. Later I found a copy of the letter Uncle Lenus had written to Father after his visit to us:

"Ralph, my dear brother, you shall never know how I felt when John called me on the phone and told me Gertrude was very sick in the hospital. We three brothers (Les and Mart coming from Wahoo) met in Springfield on Saturday evening and went to see the children. Ralph, what brave and wonderful children you have. Not one tear did I see any of them shed. We went to church with them on Sunday morning. John sang a solo. Never did he falter, but I could have cried my soul out.

"When we went to see Gertrude in the hospital, we found her in a crowded ward and insisted that she be put in a private room immediately.

"She looked up at us and smiled. 'Why did you boys come?' she asked. We told her that one of the last things we had promised you before you left was that we were no farther away than the telephone when help was needed. We wanted to see that the children had what they needed. She said, 'I have such good brothers,' and I answered, 'Well, Gertrude, we have a good sister too.' "

The next morning a letter came from my grandmother in Wahoo.

"When I heard about your mother and how sick she was, I felt numb," she wrote. "Then Les and Mart came back from Springfield. They told how terrible Gertrude looked when they saw her, but she was conscious and thanked them for coming. I went into my bedroom by myself and pleaded with my Lord for help. I asked Him to spare her if possible. I felt relieved and got the assurance that she would get well. . . ."

These words were to me as comforting as if Dr. Knabb himself had pronounced her out of danger.

To my surprise, there was also a letter from Mrs. Danielson, who was now living with her six children in Lindsborg, Kansas. She must have guessed the desperate state of our finances that month, for she enclosed a check.

Her letter reminded me that we had money problems, all right. The day Mother was admitted to the hospital, the office had asked for a down payment. Father had left her with a single blank check so that his account could be transferred to her name as soon as he sailed. But in her delirium she made the check out for five dollars and sixty cents. This was the only signed check she had. Nothing could be done now to release from Father's account the money we so desperately needed until we got word from him.

Three weeks went by. Mother's condition did not improve. Paul came to see us, bringing Mother's father, Grandfather Jacobson, with him. It was a comfort to see our oldest brother even though only for a few hours.

One night Mother asked me how long she had been in the hospital. When I told her it was almost four weeks, she couldn't believe it. To her it seemed more like two or three days.

I woke up with a start on the morning of July 9. This was Daddy's birthday! But how different it would be from our joyful celebration of last year.

I went about my usual chores at the Kollmeyers as though it were any ordinary day. I washed diapers and hung them out to dry. Then I gave the baby a bath. But my thoughts were all of Father. Where would he be? On board ship—in great danger? I consoled myself by thinking that Mother had seemed a little better last night. But she was so completely worn out. Her hair had turned white. If she had to fight any more, where would she find the strength?

I was getting supper when the telephone rang. It was John.

"Guess what Veda's fixing for us to eat tonight!" he said gleefully.

"I can't. What?"

"Fried frogs' legs."

"Ugh!"

"I went hunting bullfrogs last night in the James River."

"Well!" I retorted. "I'm glad I'm eating here."

A moment of silence.

"Ingrid, I've got news for you. Can you take it?"

My heart began to pound. I tried to sound calm as I answered:

"Yes, John, go ahead."

"We've a cablegram from Capetown."

"Is it from Daddy? What does it say? Is it bad news?"

"Wait—wait a minute. That's why I called you. There's just one word in it: 'Love,' signed 'Ralph.'"

"Then Daddy's safe! He's safe! Otherwise he *couldn't* send a cablegram. Did you call the hospital to tell Mother?"

"No, I didn't call. Gas rationing or no, I wanted to tell her myself. I went as fast as the old car could go. Mother must have read my face, for she did not seem surprised. When I told her the news, we laughed and cried together.

"Dr. Knabb walked in when I was there. He said:

"'John, I think your mother's out of danger. She's going to get well.' When Mother told him that Daddy had landed safely, he remarked to her solemnly: 'Well, Mrs. Hult, you traveled a long, dark road yourself while he was making that journey!'"

Four.

Grave in Dar

In the weeks that followed, life at Bethany Homestead was a happy time for us. Mother improved rapidly; at last the wonderful day arrived when she came home from the hospital. Although she was still quite weak, her presence among us made the world seem right again.

One morning, a few days later, we found the first letter from our father in the mailbox. Eagerly, we took it in to Mother. The very sight of the postmark on the envelope seemed to bring back memories to her.

"Think, children!" she said as her fingers tugged at the flap. "Over twenty years ago your father and I were together in Capetown. Oh, how we shivered, coming down from the sweltering climate of West Africa into the cool, bracing air of the Cape! But let's hear what Daddy has to say."

She read:

"Tomorrow we leave for up-country and Tanganyika after busy days here in Capetown. Pastor Melander and I have done a lot of walking, but it was what we needed after the trying journey across the Atlantic. Now I can tell you we were on a munitions ship, and in danger of being blown up at any moment. Yesterday, to celebrate my birthday, we took a long hike up Table Mountain. I thought of you, Gertrude, and all the memories of our visit came flooding back to me.

"I bought a very fine biography of David Livingstone in a bookstore here. We'll be traveling northward from the Cape, following almost the same route he took. One of our first stops will be at Victoria Falls which he discovered on November 17, 1855. I even have a walking cane now exactly like the one he's holding in the famous statue of him overlooking the Falls."

There was no note of sadness until the end. Then he wrote:

"Must leave here without any word. I suppose your letters are delayed somewhere, but I hoped to the last to hear from *Home*. I shall have to be patient."

It was that last paragraph which made us feel bad. To think that so far he hadn't received any of our letters—not even that airmail one to which we had all contributed. We felt like crying.

The time came to make our plans for the school year. Mother called us around her one day and announced that she had a surprise. Not only was I to go back to the Academy in Wahoo for my senior year, but Veda and Eunie were to go too, Eunie as a freshman and Veda as a sophomore. We knew that this decision took courage, for it would mean a heavy financial drain on Mother. Also, she would have only our younger brothers and sisters to help her with the chores at the Homestead. And this at a time when she had not yet recovered her strength.

But she was adamant. We three sisters were enchanted at the idea of living together in the Girls' Dorm at the Academy. We had as yet no idea what we wanted to do with our lives. But at least we were to have an education. Of course, we would have to work hard to earn our room and board, for Mother could afford to pay only for our tuition. But that didn't matter. We three girls would be going to the same school—the one our father had attended thirty years earlier—and it would be a glorious year.

Not long after we were settled at Wahoo we heard from Paul,

who was in the Marine Corps. He wrote that he was about to be sent to the Pacific. We could only pray that God would protect him. Then came word that John had been drafted and was on his way to Texas for basic training.

That left Mother all alone at the Homestead with the five younger children.

She wrote us that Carl, who was twelve, was her right-hand man. He even had to drive the old Packard until she could get her license. Carl, sitting high on a pillow and wearing an old felt hat to make him look older than his years, would take his place behind the steering wheel with Mother in the front seat beside him. Then they would set out on their weekly marketing trips to Springfield.

Mother forwarded to us another letter which had come from Father, this time postmarked Victoria Falls. He began with the first line of a hymn:

> How wondrous and great
> are Thy works, God of Praise.

He continued: "Today one of the dreams of my life has been realized. I have been privileged to *hear* and *see* the 'Mosi-oa-Tunya' ('The Smoke that Sounds') . . . Victoria Falls, which Livingstone not only discovered but also named.

"How I wish that you and I, Gertrude, might be together here someday—and that some of our children, too, may visit the place.

"Even Livingstone found it difficult to describe such an experience when he said: 'No one can imagine the beauty of the view from anything witnessed in England. *But scenes so lovely must have been gazed upon by angels in their flight.*'"

Father concluded by describing his visit to the Livingstone Museum:

"Here is housed a wonderful collection of things associated with the life and work of the great missionary-explorer. Especially interesting were the originals of letters written by Livingstone.

"In the afternoon of our last day, Melander and I walked up along the river above the Falls for a couple of miles. Perhaps you will smile when I tell you what I did there. Remember the walking stick I told you about buying in Capetown which was an exact replica of the one on Livingstone's statue? Well, I took it and christened it in the waters of the Zambesi, the great river which he explored."

Letters followed now in quick succession after having been two and three months on their way. One of them was written on the deck of a lake steamer.

"After our river journey on the Lualaba, we are now crossing Lake Tanganyika. This reminds us again of our ocean journey, with the difference, however, that here we have no fears of submarines or mines. . . . How wonderful when this terrible war is over and the ships of the world can again move from port to port without fear of destruction by some enemy.

"I just sent a message to you all with the setting sun. You were so near to me as I looked out toward the west. I shall be doing that often—sending messages to my loved ones at *Home* with the setting sun—or moon. Suppose you realize that when it is 6 P.M. here it is about noon at home with you.

"Looking out toward the mountains on the southeastern shoreline is so interesting to me because David Livingstone traveled through them on his way to and from Ujiji. You remember that is the place where Stanley found him. Livingstone had come to Ujiji in the hope of finding letters from home. How disappointed he was when he found none! But when he came there a second time, more dead than alive, he met Stanley who had not only letters but also much-needed supplies of medicine, food, and clothing.

"Speaking of letters, I wonder if I shall find any for me when we reach Ruruma. It is now two months since I left. It seems much longer. So many things could have happened in that time. I do hope my letters will reach you, so you will know that all is well with me. It still seems almost like a dream that I'm back in Africa after all these years of absence. God has indeed been good to us."

The school year progressed. I was no longer lonesome at the Academy with both Veda and Eunie there, too. We looked forward to Sundays when we could visit our grandmother and read Father's letters to her.

One day he wrote that he had reached Mashame, the station on the slopes of Mount Kilimanjaro which he considered the most beautiful spot in the world. We knew that this must mean much to him, for it was there that he and Mother had served when they first arrived in Tanganyika.

It was at Mashame, he said, that he received his first letters from home. That was when he learned of Mother's illness, but happily, the same mail brought word of her recovery, and her own handwritten note to him which ended with this sentence: "How thankful I have been that I did not get sick until after you left, Ralph, because otherwise it might have prevented your leaving. I am always thanking God that you can at last be in Africa."

Father wrote that those words were a great consolation to him, for the first thing that had occurred to him upon learning of her illness was that she might have been sorry that she let him go.

From another letter to Mother:

"How memories flock together these days at Mashame! It is a thrill to come back after so many years and find African Christians who still remember us.

"Every time I go in and out of this house I am reminded of days gone by. I see my Gertrude moving about the rooms and about the mission grounds. I see little Paulo and his chubby brother Yohane—even baby Ingridi. I can see their little sister Ruth, who spent such a short while with us before leaving for a better home.

"The first thing I did after I arrived here was to visit the cemetery and to stand there beside our precious little grave. It did my heart good. It was so peaceful there on the mountainside. I imagined you at my side, Gertrude, and I asked you all the questions in my heart. . . .

"How different everything would be for me now, if we could have carried on in Africa together all these years. Why should we have been cut off from the tasks we so much loved? . . . But I hope and pray that we still have something to do in the missionary work of today. *And where our work shall end, may our children carry on.*"

Eunie and Veda and I looked at one another. From the time we were little girls, Eunie always said she wanted to be a mother, but instead of having only ten children, her goal was twenty. Veda had known that she wanted to be a nurse, and I, a teacher. But where? For the first time a new thought came to us. Would our work be on the mission field?

Then we received news of Father's assignment. He had been appointed superintendent of the Usaramo District, a territory so large it was formerly served by at least a score of missionaries. Now Father would have to handle it alone.

He was to be stationed at Dar es Salaam, the capital of Tanganyika and one of its main ports. Dar was considered a "hardship post," for the climate was steaming, and at that time disease was rampant. Father did not mind, so great was his happiness at being once more in the work.

"I have arrived at Dar at the beginning of the hot season," he wrote us. "You can imagine how I perspire in this sticky heat. . . . I try to get enough sleep, though it is difficult in the heat of the night—and one never wakens refreshed. I walk to the waterfront early in the morning and again in the evening. It is so refreshing to get even slight breezes from off the water. . . . At times I am almost sick with my longing to see you and be with you. . . . It is now five months since the last letter I received from you was written—July 23."

It made our hearts ache, for we had faithfully answered each one of his, telling him about our activities, of the fine year we were having at the Academy. We had enclosed snapshots of us and clippings from the school paper.

We were looking forward to the Spring Youth Conference to be held in March. One of our speakers was to be a missionary from Africa, Mrs. George Anderson, and we knew Father would enjoy hearing about that. Young people were to join us from all parts of Nebraska.

Our Youth Conference was everything we expected. There was a feeling of spring in the air the following Monday morning. The last traces of snow were melting away. I was resting between classes in my room. In a few minutes the bell would ring for our ten o'clock period. Suddenly, I heard a knock on the door.

"Come in," I called out without bothering to get up. I was startled to see Pastor Lauersen, our new president, standing in the doorway. I was even more alarmed when I saw that Veda and Eunie were with him. Why should he be here in the Girls' Dorm? What was wrong?

In a flash I thought of that other Monday morning, just two years ago, when Dr. Lindberg had stopped me on the stairs of Old Main and called me into his office. Then it was to tell me the news of the sinking of the *Zamzam*. What would it be this time? I felt it even before he told us.

President Lauersen was solemn.

"I wanted you girls to be all together before I say what I have to say," he declared.

We exchanged glances.

"A cablegram has just been received from Dar es Salaam. Your father passed away from heart failure following malaria on March 18."

He had broken it to us as gently as he could.

That other time I had said to myself: "I know my father's not dead. He's alive. I'll see him again."

But this time I knew with a great finality that my father was dead.

This was the greatest blow of my life.

I think I might have fainted had I not felt that countless arms of love were upholding me. I was aware of the reservoirs of a new strength—something that I had never before experienced. Veda and Eunie wept almost hysterically at the first shock of the news. But as we fell into each other's arms, we knew a great comfort, a comfort from outside ourselves.

Pastor Lauersen continued:

"Your mother, down in Springfield alone with your five youngest brothers and sisters, has not heard. You're the one who must tell her, Ingrid. Your Uncle Mart is here, waiting to take you to your grandmother's home. She will need you, too. You will also need her this day," he said.

We found our grandmother with tears in her eyes, yet her face was serene. Uncle Mart had already told her of the cablegram.

"It's no surprise to me," she said. "Strange, but for these last days I have known in my heart that Ralph was no longer on this earth." She looked up then at his picture. It was hanging above a photograph of her husband, who also had died unexpectedly when he was in his early fifties. "It makes me long all the more to be with them in heaven," she said with a sigh. Tomorrow would be her seventy-ninth birthday.

From my grandmother's house I called Mother at the Homestead. She answered the phone and greeted me with her usual cheeriness.

"Mother," I said, "I have some bad news for you."

"Yes, Ingrid, tell me what it is," she said slowly.

I read her the cablegram we had received from the mission office. There was a long moment of silence. Then she asked me in a normal voice how we were; she was especially concerned about Grandmother.

I learned later what a hard day it had been for her. Carl was sick with the measles, and the other children were coming down with them. Also, she had two hundred baby chicks to care for. She simply had no time to give herself over to grief, and as she

wrote us, perhaps this was her greatest help in enduring the shock
of the news.

When she came to Wahoo for the memorial service for Father,
I tried to think of some way to comfort her. She answered me
simply:

"You do not yet realize, Ingrid, what it means to lose your life
partner."

The word of my father's death had a great impact on the
Academy. In his first class that Monday, Pastor Lauersen let the
news be known to the older students. A hushed silence followed.
Then he said:

"The day on which Pastor Hult died was March 18, the first
day of our Youth Conference. His name was often mentioned in
our sessions, although we did not know of his death. It was here
that he first heard the call to Africa and dedicated his life to
becoming a missionary. Now he is dead. Who will carry on where
he left off?"

Ten of the young men in that class raised their hands and came
forward while the others bowed their heads in prayer. Of those
ten, seven would eventually become foreign missionaries, the
other three, pastors here at home.

The regular meeting of our Missionary Society was scheduled
for March 27. Veda, Eunie, and I would be in charge of the
program, and also responsible for a survey of each of our three
mission fields, Africa, China, and India. We had accepted our
assignments before we heard the news of our father's death.

With the meeting only a few days away, I happened to meet
the head of the society one morning on the steps of Old Main.

"You don't have to go through with it, Ingrid," he said gently,
"if you don't feel like it. We can get someone else to take your
place. Everyone will understand."

We talked it over among ourselves. Veda was fifteen, and
Eunie, thirteen. Finally, we agreed that since we were prepared
and also since it would be a chance to share publicly with others
our feeling about our father's death, we should go ahead. I, as the

oldest, would be the spokesman, although we had worked out our message together.

All too soon the moment of testing came. I still remember all those faces swimming before me in the brightly lighted chapel auditorium.

"Before closing, I would like to say a few words about my father." I had a hard time keeping my voice steady. "As you know, his whole life was dedicated to the mission field, and especially to the challenge of Africa.

"It was right here, in this very school, when he was eighteen that he dedicated his life to that cause. Now God has seen fit to take him away.

"It is hard to understand why he should be taken now, when he was so badly needed in Tanganyika, and when it seems that he was in the prime of his life and best equipped to serve his Master. But we know that God always has a reason and someday we shall understand. We refuse to give way to grief. Rather, we count it a duty and a privilege to carry on God's work where Father left off.

"My sisters and I are now more determined than ever to give our lives entirely to the expansion of God's Kingdom here on earth, in the manner and place which to Him seems best."

There was a hush over the auditorium as I sat down.

We made this pledge sincerely out of the earnestness of our youthful hearts.

But were we ready? Could we keep our promises? Did we really know whereof we spoke?

Five.

The Green Trunk

That summer in Wahoo I got my first job as secretary to the president of the Academy. It pleased me that I could take care of myself.

But I was worried about what the future held for Mother. Paul and John were away in the service. The others were growing up. The rocky acres of the Homestead could barely produce a living. If the situation caused Mother some anxious hours, however, she never let us know.

Then suddenly came an answer. Mother wrote that the Academy had invited her to become librarian and also instructor in English.

The offer propounded a problem. It would be necessary for Mother to give up her home where she had lived for fourteen years. Futhermore, twenty years had now passed since she graduated from college—twenty years which she had spent as a housewife and mother. Would she be able to resume her intellectual activities after such a period?

On the other hand, if she moved to Wahoo she would at least be able to keep a home together and pay for the children's education.

In the end Mother accepted. In preparation she attended summer school at Springfield Teachers College. She arranged to rent the Homestead at the beginning of the school year and move to Wahoo. One fine morning she set out in the Packard, the children in their accustomed places, all her household goods trundling along in the trailer behind.

In Wahoo we found a house next to the campus. Once more we hung the big map of Africa on the wall, and in general tried to make it as much like the Homestead as possible.

We named our house Dar es Salaam (which means Haven of Peace) and hung over the couch in the living room, the picture of the palm-studded harbor where our father died. But with all nine of us (Mother included) in school and all trying to do our homework around the dining-room table, it was far from being a haven of any kind.

We hadn't been in our new home very long when Mother was asked to be counselor for the Students' Missionary Society. This work seemed to mean a great deal to her. She took her new responsibilities very seriously.

Mother surprised us one night by announcing that she was planning to add to her activities by enrolling the next school year in a college Spanish course.

The months went by. Paul and John were mustered out of the service. In the summer of 1946 came the first wedding in the family. We were pleased when Paul married Ann Evans, a lovely girl from Philadelphia and a graduate of Temple University. He continued his studies there, working in a garage at night. John went on to medical school in St. Louis.

I began to notice that Mother was often abstracted, increasingly absorbed in her own thoughts. One night she let me know what was on her mind.

"Ingrid," she said, "I can't go on doing it any longer."

"Doing what?"

"Keep urging these fine young people to go to the mission field unless I'm willing to go myself."

I was startled.

"I didn't know you had anything like that in mind," I said.

"Yes, always," Mother replied. "I didn't give up hope for a long time that someday I might go back to Africa with your father. Now, of course, I can never do that. But I'm still thinking there must be someplace where I can serve when you children no longer need me."

As she talked on, she disclosed that this was the reason for her interest in Spanish. Now it seemed justified. Only recently she had read of a young mission in La Paz, Bolivia, which was in desperate need of a matron for the orphanage there.

"I've been trying to forget it," Mother said, "but I confess I seem unable to do so. Perhaps this is the place I've been looking for where I could serve. I could be a mother to those twenty-six motherless little ones. But before I do anything, I want to talk it over with you children. This has to be a family decision."

We had a number of councils around the dining-room table. Mother wrote to Paul and John. In the end we agreed that she should go.

And so it was that in the fall of 1947, four years after Father's death, Mother, then almost fifty, stood one evening before the congregation in our church in Wahoo to be commissioned for service in Bolivia. She told the audience:

"The other day I saw a newborn baby. It made me sad that I couldn't start all over again and raise another family. But then, I thought of the little ones in the world who have no mother. Perhaps I could serve by mothering them.

"I had been reading about the orphanage on Coaba Farm, where there are twenty-six children to care for. So I wrote to Mr. Lindell, the mission director. My application has been accepted.

"I pondered this call for many months. But what about my own children? you may very well ask. Don't they still need me? Do you know where I finally found the answer? In the words of Isaiah: 'Enlarge the place of thy tent, and let them stretch forth the curtains of thy habitations. . . . *And all thy children shall*

be taught of the Lord; and great shall be the peace of thy children'
[54:2, 13].

"This is the way I've got it worked out:

"Gustav, thirteen, will go to live with my brother Verne and
his wife Lula, in Geneseo. It will be good for Gus to have someone who can be a father to him. The others will continue their
studies. My children are behind me in this decision. And as to my
two youngest, David, nine, and Mary, eleven? I'll tell you—they
will go with me.

"Just a few weeks ago I became a grandmother for the first
time. My oldest son, Paul, and his wife, Ann, had a baby girl.
But, you know, I'm convinced that this business of carrying the
Gospel to all the world is so important that even we grandmothers have to go!"

She sat down, leaving the audience silent, stunned by the
impact of her declaration.

I helped Mother close up our home in Wahoo. Then I drove
back with her to the Homestead, which was now unoccupied.

As we headed southward hour after hour, we passed the time
talking things over.

"Mother," I asked her at one point, "wasn't it a great sacrifice
for you to have ten children?"

She looked at me in amazement. She became so excited that
she raised her foot from the gas pedal, almost stopping the car.

"Why, Ingrid, that was no sacrifice!" she exclaimed. "I consider it the highest honor God could give me—to be the mother of
the children of Ralph Hult. I'd always prayed for a large family,
because that's the way I thought I could best serve my Lord—by
being a mother. When we had only five children, and I saw
you all healthy and doing well in school, well—I just asked God
for five more!"

We were so deep in our discussion that when we reached the
outskirts of Kansas City, we missed the bypass and drove right
into the heart of downtown. All about us cars tooted disdainfully.

Our Packard, with its back seat loaded to the top, and pulling the trailer on which teetered the well-worn Maytag filled with potatoes, retained hardly a trace of its former dignity. Mother calmly made all the complicated turns until we were outside the city. Then she pulled over to the side of the road, stretched out on a blanket under the nearest shade tree, and took a nap before going on to Springfield.

As we resumed driving, we discussed what was going to happen to the Homestead when Mother went to Bolivia. It was then that she confided to me that with Father's insurance money, she had paid off the last debt. Oh what this meant to me! All through my childhood the mortgage had hung over us. After years of struggling, we now had a clear title to the farm.

My parents had often wished that others might enjoy the beauty and quiet restfulness of Bethany Homestead. Now Mother disclosed her plan: It would be just the place for missionaries on furlough to regain their strength, for tired Christian workers to go to for a vacation. I shared her enthusiasm.

With this purpose in mind, Mother later signed papers relinquishing her ownership. Friends all over the country sent in donations. A corporation was formed, making Bethany Homestead a Christian rest home and place for quiet retreats. At a great financial sacrifice Pastor and Mrs. C. O. Carlson gave up their parish in Nebraska to direct the project.

I had only a few days' vacation left before the fall school term. I planned to help Mother get the place ready. I would sort out Father's books and papers, and the family possessions, before we turned the Homestead over to its new occupants.

I tackled the boys' cottage. Old furniture, clothing, and odds and ends that had been stored there would have to be gone through to see what should be saved, and what thrown away.

Outside the autumn air was crisp and clear on the morning I set to work. A few brown leaves still clung to the oak trees, but the maples were bare. Their leaves had long since fallen to form a golden carpet on the lane. I would have much preferred to be out tramping in the woods, but I kept at it. Suddenly, buried under a heap of old magazines, I discovered a little green tin trunk.

It caught my imagination. What was in it? I pulled it out and brought it over to the light. There, painted in white on the top and on both ends, I saw the initials R.D.H. My father's trunk! The sides were still covered with steamship stickers. By now I was consumed with curiosity. I had to see what was inside.

I cleared a place on the cluttered floor, then sat down beside the chest. I opened the lid excitedly. The trunk contained my father's journals.

On top were those he had written as a student; then the ones he had kept on his first trip to Africa. Yes, here were the maps he had made of his travels, painstakingly drawn; the word lists of each tribe he had visited; letters to and from the mission board; and piles of old yellow clippings. Where had the trunk been all this time? How had it come here? Why, he must have packed it and arranged the contents so carefully on one of his last days at home.

I trembled as I unpacked the journals and sorted them out. I thought I knew my father—but *did* I know him, really? Here before me was the record of his life and thoughts over the years, set down in his own hand. I felt that I was about to discover him for the first time. I leaned my back against a chair and began to read:

"I was born in Kearney, Nebraska, at that time a little frontier town on the prairies. Until I started school, I could only speak Swedish, for all my grandparents as well as my mother were born in Sweden. Although my father had been born in New Sweden, Iowa, he found it hard to believe that God spoke anything but Swedish.

"I was the oldest child in the family, and according to my mother's reports, was very adventurous. One day before I was three I found my way across the prairies to the railroad tracks a mile from our home. The train for Denver came roaring by. I waved for it to stop; but the engineer just waved back at me.

A few minutes later my father came galloping up on his horse. My anxious parents had been searching for me in all directions. My joy at seeing him made me forget my disappointment in not being able to go away on the big train with my little dog. But when I learned to read I no longer wanted to run away from home, for I could escape into the world of books.

"One day I saw an ad in the *Youth's Companion* describing a pressure can with a guage, which registered the power of your lungs when you blew into the tube. I wanted to order it, but I had no money. I showed the advertisement to my father.

" 'Why do you want it, Ralph?' he asked.

" 'If I am going to become a minister, I must have strong lungs so I can preach loud,' I answered.

"He gave me the money.

"My happiest childhood memories were of the Lind family reunions at my grandparents' sod house just north of Funk, Nebraska. Especially 'Julskapet,' our Christmas party. We had a glorious time, all we cousins running and playing outside.

"I finished grade school. It was a great disappointment that I couldn't start high school right away, but Father needed me on the farm. Four long years I waited before I could pack my trunk and set out for our church high school, Luther Academy in Wahoo. I dreamed a lot those years about the future as I walked up and down the fields, plowing corn, preparing the wheat fields, bringing in the harvest. . . ."

I put the journal down. I had not realized that the delays and disappointments which marked my father's life began so early. Yet it must have been from those same hard experiences that he learned the secret of waiting in patience.

I read on . . .

"But the day came. Father drove me in our wagon over the rutted prairie roads to Kearney where I would take the train for Wahoo.

"As we stood waiting on the train platform, he handed me a small black book—a Swedish New Testament. Then as he bade me good-by he said: 'You're eighteen and a man now, Ralph. Always remember the first Psalm. . . .'

"How happy I was at Luther Academy! Everything in me responded as I sat in the classrooms of this fine school, built on the highest hill in Wahoo, a monument to the Swedish pioneers who built it, and to their faith in higher education.

"On Sunday evening, April 14, of that year 1907, I mounted the polished wooden stairs to the chapel on the third floor of Old Main. A pastor from a neighboring church, Fred Wyman, was to speak that evening at a meeting of the Missionary Society. His topic was: 'Sudan—the Greatest Unevangelized Field in the World.'

"Pastor Wyman talked to us about that great area in central Africa where one could travel thousands of miles without finding a single mission station. From his first sentence to his last, my heart was strangely gripped. Islam was coming down from the North. Who would reach these hundreds of pagan tribes first? Would it be Christ or Mohammed? And he closed with the plea from Isaiah 6:8: 'Whom shall I send, and who will go for us?'

"The meeting over, I slipped quickly out of the chapel. Before going to my dormitory room I had to fight this out alone. I went into the cornfield next to the campus, and paced back and forth. Then I looked up at the stars on that clear, spring evening and gave God my answer: 'Here am I! Lord, send me.'

"I wasn't dismayed that I had ten years of school ahead before I could be ordained. I could use that time to learn about the Sudan.

"Just a few months later my parents decided to move to Wahoo. My father was on the Academy Board and he wanted all of his children to be educated there. Then tragedy struck our family. That fall my father went back to our farm in western Nebraska to market the grain. He borrowed a team of horses from his neighbor and was on his way to town with a load of wheat which he had pledged to missions. Something frightened the horses, so that they bolted and ran away.

"Father was thrown from the wagon and hurt internally. He came back to Wahoo, but grew steadily worse. When he knew he was dying, he called his five sons and three daughters to his bedside. He put his hand in blessing on each of us, even my two-year-old brother Lenus, and then he asked for us to sing to him in Swedish his favorite hymn, 'Rock of Ages':

> 'While I draw this fleeting breath,
> When my eyelids close in death . . .
> Rock of ages, cleft for me.
> Let me hide myself in Thee.'

"I was nineteen and the oldest son. My father, always so strong and vital, was gone. It was up to me to take his place.

"What a sad day when I trudged up the hill to the Academy and President Johnson's office. I had come to tell him I must give up my studies for the year. Instead of reading, I would again be walking behind a plow. Dreams of Africa would remain—only dreams."

How intense must have been his vision that he could have the strength and courage to go on! My eye skipped quickly to the next paragraphs.

"Thanks to my mother's sacrifices, I was able to go back to school. In June, 1910, just a few weeks before my twenty-second birthday, I graduated. Luther Academy had done a good job on us. Of the ten boys in my class, all of us became either pastors or missionaries. The two girls both married pastors.

"The next fall I entered Augustana College at Rock Island. There I met Dr. Kumm, founder of the Sudan United Mission, who was on a lecture tour. Everything he said was fuel to the fire which burned within me. Among the stories he told was one concerning a great German missionary, Johann Ludwig Krapf. He and his partner, Johannes Rebmann, were the first white men to discover Mount Kilimanjaro. Dr. Kumm described how Dr. Krapf had envisioned a chain of mission stations extending clear across the continent. Dr. Krapf's last words as he lay dying were particularly inspiring to me. He said: 'Though I fall, it does not matter; for the Lord will carry on and complete His cause in His own good time. . . . The idea is always conceived tens of years before the deed comes to pass.'

"I wanted so much to help carry out Dr. Krapf's vision. This desire was also shared by other student volunteers.

"We began meeting regularly to study the needs of the Sudan and to pray earnestly that our Church might see the urgency of sending someone out to this field in need.

"After finishing college, I still had three years left of theological studies before I could be ordained. In 1917 a sophomore named Gertrude Jacobson joined our Student Volunteer Band. I was attracted to her from the first—not so much by her beauty as by her refreshing naturalness, her enthusiasm and her energy.

"I had long considered the choice of a partner as one of the most important steps in life—one to be taken only under divine guidance. In my summer work, which was selling books, I had been inside of literally hundreds of homes in the United States. But I had never met a girl who so nearly corresponded to my ideal of what a wife should be.

"I'll never forget the morning I asked her for our first date. She was coming down the steps of Old Main after the morning chapel service, her arms full of books. Wearing a white middy blouse over her tan skirt, her chestnut-colored hair piled high on her head, she looked at me in great surprise as I stopped her at the bottom of the stairs.

" 'Miss Jacobson, may I have a word with you?' I said.

"And then I asked her if she would go with me that evening to hear Judge Ben Lindsay at the Lyceum series. She was only eighteen, her merry girlishness ripening into full, rich womanhood. I was ten years her senior, but on our first date that evening of April 13, 1917, any doubts that I might have entertained, disappeared. I knew that she was the girl for me.

"We had many long walks and talks together and it did not take us long to realize that we were in love. But what about the future? That would be decided when our church body met for its annual convention in June.

"The moment for which I had been preparing was now at hand. Our church had a mission field in India and in China, but none in Africa. The Augustana College Missionary Society had recommended to our church convention that we begin a mission in Africa. On June 14 the issue came up for discussion. The church president asked me to take the floor and tell the hundreds of delegates in the auditorium about the great need in the Sudan. I spoke out of an overflowing heart—in Swedish, for that was the language of the convention. The issue was put to a vote. Like a great thunder in the auditorium came the resounding Swedish *Ja*—and not a single dissenting vote.

"And then three days later, I was ordained and commissioned as the first missionary of the Augustana Lutheran Church to Africa with orders to begin work in the Sudan. That same evening under 'our' tree on the campus, I asked Gertrude to become my wife. She accepted. There was not a doubt in our hearts but that God had led us together and that He wanted us to serve Him together. I had saved my money to buy her engagement ring. Inside it was engraved 'Psalm 67:1, 2,' the prayer of our life together.

"We weren't married until two years afterward. She had just graduated from Augustana College, one of only four girls in her class of forty. In the meantime I had graduated from the Kennedy School of Missions in Hartford, Connecticut. Our wedding was a simple one. We were married in the living room of Gertrude's home. Our dreams were about to come true. . . ."

Dreams, I thought to myself. Wasn't my father's life just a series of dreams—dreams almost, but never quite, fulfilled in his lifetime?

I paged through the black leather journal for 1919 written in my father's characteristically neat, but bold, handwriting. I came to an entry made just three months after their wedding.

Another disappointment! The mission board had decided it

would be best for my father to go out alone to make his first journeys of exploration . . .

He wrote:

"Gertrude and I stand on the platform of the Rock Island station for our last minutes together. We had been up late the night before, packing my trunk for Africa. Now Father and Mother Jacobson look on helplessly as we struggle to overcome our emotion.

"A train whistle! Only a few more seconds and I will be on my way to New York, across the Atlantic, down the west coast of Africa, landing in Nigeria, going by river boat up the Benoué . . . then trekking for days, months, in search of that tribe where God has called me to be the first witness, while here I must leave my bride. When would we see each other again? In one year? Two years? . . ."

Pages of travelogue followed. He described the supreme moment when, after fifteen days at sea, he caught his first glimpse of Africa:

"I was up long before dawn as our ship docked in Dakar. I could see the lights of land blinking in the darkness. Then the black outline of earth meeting sea. In a moment it was gray—not gradually, but suddenly. I thought, nothing stops this advance of light, once the dawn begins—just as if a curtain had been raised. 'Daybreak in the Dark Continent.'"

At Lagos, Nigeria, he left the ship. He traveled more than a thousand miles, first up the Niger River, then the Benoué, finally reaching Garoua, the port of entry to northern Cameroun.

The orderly sequence of journals came to an abrupt end. Evidently there had been no time for recording impressions once he began his arduous journey eastward on foot. Had he left no record of his first contact with the primitive life in this region? Then I noticed a packet of loose sheets neatly numbered and labeled, "My Sudan Journey." On these in pencil he had made his notes during that six-month trek. I fell upon them eagerly.

The page on top was dated December 11, 1920. For three

months he had stayed in Garoua, studying Fulani. During that time he had become very ill with dysentery. Loneliness only increased his suffering. More than six months had passed since he heard from Gertrude, then in Omaha taking special medical training.

I read another sheet:

"I looked back and watched Garoua vanish behind the hills. We were ten in our little caravan—seven porters carrying supplies, a horseboy, my cook, Alfons, and myself. Somewhere in this region I will find the tribe where we could begin our mission."

And so he had gone on, visiting twenty different tribes. Each evening he sat at his little camp table and by the light of a candle or kerosene lantern wrote down his impressions of the day, and detailed maps of his route.

I picked up the packet of word lists. To study the lingual relationships of the various tribes, he took one hundred of the most commonly used words and sought to find their equivalent in each tribe.

But still he did not find the tribe to which he had been called.

Then one day he stopped for supplies at an outpost named Fort Archambault. He fell into conversation with a government official there, who told him of a remarkable tribe, the Saras.

"These fine people are physically strong, intelligent, and unusually industrious," the government man said. "But they are still pagans, and show little tolerance for the Moslems who, for generations, have raided their country for slaves."

Father felt the Saras ought to become Christians. He went at once in search of the tribe. He found them much as they had been described.

"I spent over two months in the Sara country," Father wrote. "At night I listened to the tom-toms in the distance. Then even before breakfast, visitors would come to my door—often the chief of the village with his elders. I told them the old, old story and they listened. 'No one told us anything like that before,' they would say. 'You are a God-man. I shall tell these words to my children.'

"In my mind now there was no doubt. God was calling us to work here. I prepared a report for the Home Board and sent a cablegram: 'SARA PEOPLE WAITING.' I even marked the site where our first station could be built."

On the next page was a story about the king who sent him a beautiful white Arabian horse.

" 'You entered my town on a little pagan pony, but I cannot have a servant of Allah leave in that way,' the king said. I replied that the pony was quite good enough for me, but he would not hear of my refusal to accept his gift. He sent me a second message:

" 'The horse is not given to you, but to Allah. If you, as Allah's servant, refuse to accept it, I will order it to be led into the bush, to be tied to a tree and left there to be eaten by wild animals.' Naturally, I took it."

The main narrative resumed:

"Now I could bring Gertrude to this place, so we might begin together the work of bringing the Gospel to the Sara people."

From there I was familiar with the story: how he had retraced his steps on foot and on horseback to Garoua, then down the Benoué in a river boat.

At Numan, Nigeria, starved all these months for news, he found letter after letter from Gertrude. One had special significance. While he was on his long trip of exploration, she had arrived in Nigeria! She was staying at Wukari, waiting to hear from him.

Late in the evening of June 8, 1921, Gertrude was getting ready for bed in the hut where she was living, when she heard the crunch of footsteps on the gravel outside.

Surely she knew that step—but no, it wasn't possible. Someone knocked on her door.

"Who's there?" she called, a little frightened.

"Ralph."

She cried aloud. After almost two years of separation, she was in her husband's arms.

They prepared to return together to the Saras. What detailed plans they made as to how they would build that first station! Many hours were spent discussing the equipment they would need. While they waited for word from home, granting them permission to begin, they worked at Kwona, Nigeria, a station of the Sudan United Mission.

Then one day, several months later, a cablegram came from the home office. It said simply:

"GO TO TANGANYIKA."

Only three words. But those words would change the whole course of their lives.

Father was dismayed when he heard he could not go to the tribe to which he felt called. But he was aware of the great need in Tanganyika where so many German missionaries had been sent home because of World War I and could not return. In the end, like a good soldier, he decided to obey orders and cabled his board:

"CAN SEE THAT NEED JUSTIFIES MY TRANSFER."

He began making plans for the long trip.

But the needs of the Sara tribe lay heavy on his heart. He cabled to his friend, Missionary Gunderson, who was studying in Paris:

"MY BOARD CABLES 'GO TO TANGANYIKA.' WHAT ABOUT SARAS?"

While he was in Capetown, en route with Gertrude and little Paul, he compiled a report which he sent out to fifty missionary societies in Europe and in America, in the hope that surely one of them would give heed.

Then he went on to Tanganyika with his family. The years passed. They had been stationed first at Mashame, then at Old Moshi, both on the slopes of Mount Kilimanjaro.

Finally they returned home on furlough. While they were in the States, the church decided that it could not support missionary work both in the Sudan and in Tanganyika. Therefore, it would give up the Sudan.

The next year Father traveled most of the time, lecturing on his experiences, while the family lived in Wahoo. He received no word from the board as to his future work.

During this period of suffering and indecision, Veda was born. I remembered now the significance of her name, Veda Anaiah, "I know God has heard."

Father's furlough was up. He hardly expected to be called again to the Sudan and to the Saras. But to his surprise and consternation he was not called to return to Tanganyika either. There was no word of any kind. Just silence—a silence that would last for fifteen years.

A strange sequence of events led Father to Springfield, Missouri. He was in St. Louis on a speaking tour when he discovered he had some free time in his schedule. The national headquarters of the Assembly of God Church was in Springfield, and he had heard that they were beginning mission work in the Sudan. So on an impulse he took the train to Springfield. Looking out the train window, there was something about the rolling hills, the worn-off mountains, even the small trees of the Ozarks country which reminded him of Africa.

It was not hard for him, therefore, to accept a call to a small Swedish Lutheran congregation at Verona, Missouri, some months later. There Eunie was born . . .

I searched deeper in the little trunk. At the bottom of it I discovered something strange and unexpected: a large rolled-up poster—a circus poster of two African women from the Ubangi-Shari country, wearing their great lip discs. Yes, I could remember that day in Verona when Father announced that he was taking Paul and John to see the circus in Springfield. I was considered too young to go along. These pitiful women were the main attraction. They were from the very tribe in West Africa that he had longed to serve!

Afterward, while passing a real estate office in Springfield, he saw a forty-acre fruit farm on Blackman Road just east of town advertised for sale. It had belonged to Professor Chalfant, a beloved music teacher at Drury College.

Father fell in love with the farm at first sight. If he could not return to the Sudan—and now the doors seemed definitely closed —he would do his best to make a home here for himself and for his family. He arranged for a loan to buy the property. We moved there in the fall of 1930. We acquired the Homestead just in time, for meanwhile the little congregation in Verona had affiliated with a larger one in the same town, and Father was without a church.

I recall so vividly the years that followed—the Depression years. How glad we were then that we had the farm! It was ideal for us children. We enjoyed to the full all the freedom of its forty acres, the woods, the spring, the cows, the orchard. Father alone bore the burden, silently and without complaint, of trying to find a way to support his family. He sold books from door to door, and used to tell us he relished the contacts it brought him as he visited neighboring homes.

But the day came when people had no more money for books. Father did not know which way to turn. He dreamed of starting a small congregation in Springfield, and kept writing letters about it to the home missions secretary. But he always received the answer that there were no funds for such a project.

After several months without anything to do, he got a job on a WPA road gang out on the highway going toward Rogersville east of our home. He was glad to have it.

One morning, after he had gone to work, we children spied a shiny new car coming up our driveway. Who could it be? We hurried to straighten up the living room. Mother put on a clean apron and went to the door to greet our visitor. We noticed at once that he was wearing a clerical collar and a fine dark suit. Mother whispered that she recognized him as an official of the home missions board of our church. We felt that big things were about to happen.

"Where is Pastor Hult?" the visitor inquired.

Mother explained that he was not expected home until evening.

"But I can't wait that long," he said. "Can you tell me where he is working, so I can go and see him?"

Mother explained with some reluctance how to get to the Rogersville highway. The pastor left. Now we were certain that something wonderful was coming Daddy's way.

That evening when Father came home in his faded blue overalls and carrying his lunch pail, we were all waiting for him. Over our supper of bread and bacon gravy, he told what happened.

When the men on the road gang saw the shiny new car, one of them called out "Big shot!" which meant "Everybody get busy!"

The "big shot" asked the foreman if he might speak to Pastor Hult. The men just looked at one another. It was their first inkling that they had a clergyman among them. Father stepped forward.

"I'm Pastor Hult," he said quietly. The visitor drew him to one side.

A few minutes later the car drove away and Father returned to his pick and shovel. Daddy spared us the end of the story, keeping it to himself. Mother told us later who the man was in the shiny car. He had come in person to tell Daddy that there were no funds for starting a congregation in Springfield.

We reached the point where there wasn't money even to buy gas for the car. One night Father walked all the way home from town, carrying a heavy bundle. It was the week before Christmas and we were dying to know what was in it. But we had to wait until Christmas Eve, which was always a marvelously happy time. There were packages from kind relatives and friends for every one of us. But most of all we couldn't wait to see what was in the big one about which Father was so mysterious.

His eyes twinkled as he prepared to reveal it, explaining that it was one gift for us all. And there it was—a ten-volume set bound in green leather—the *Junior Classics!* He had found it at a bargain when he was poking around in the secondhand bookstores, and instead of a Christmas treat for our table, he had chosen this. The set was given a place of honor atop the reed organ. We older children soon devoured it greedily from cover to cover . . .

I shook myself out of this reverie and continued going through the packet.

Here were some old clippings from the *Springfield News and Leader*. I smiled to myself as I looked at the first one, dated April, 1936. "Healthiest Family in Greene County," it was entitled, and there we sat four brothers, four sisters—four blonds, four redheads (it was before David and Mary were born)—on a grassy bank in Fassnight Park where we had all been given awards at the annual Health Day celebration.

Father went to the newspaper office and got about twenty copies of the article which he sent to his relatives. I guess he wanted to show them we weren't just skin and bones, as they must have thought from our being raised on those barren acres. But the real credit was Mother's. By canning great quantities of fruit and vegetables each year, supplemented by our own milk and eggs, she had managed to keep her large family healthy on a shoestring budget.

Perhaps her greatest feat was keeping us supplied with protein. We could afford only half a pound of bacon a week. By cutting it into squares, frying it, adding a tablespoon of flour, mixing that with cold milk, she'd have a skillet of gravy for our potatoes or bread. Our Sunday treat was meatballs made from a pound of hamburger mixed with an onion, an egg, and two cups of bread-crumbs.

Clothing was simpler. Each of us had at least one cousin about our size, so we never lacked for things to wear. I never wore a new store dress until after I'd gone to work. Shoes were more difficult because we outgrew them so fast. But in warm weather we went barefoot.

And this other clipping? Oh yes, it had been a feature article in the Sunday paper that same July entitled: "Songs of Africa Echo on a Sunny Ozarks Farm."

I still remembered the afternoon that the reporter, Docia Karrell, had come to interview Father. We children, all barefoot, and wearing clean but well-worn clothing, had crowded around his chair as he answered her questions. I now read the article again:

"On a sunny hillside farm east of Springfield, half-a-mile from the Blackman School, a gentle and patient man dreams of Africa.

"He looks upon his parched and stony acres, and dreams of that prairie-grass, taller than a man, that waves under the hot winds of the Sudan.

"He looks upon his sturdy blond children, and though they certainly come first in his life, he dreams of needy African children half-around-the-world away.

"He sits in his attractive cobblestone cottage, and dreams of the grass-and-clay hut that native tribesmen built for him at Kwona long ago . . .

"Happy, no doubt, in his Ozarks home, Mr. Hult is still haunted sometimes by the words of the Sara chief:

" 'We have heard the name of Allah, but we do not know how to speak to Him.'

"He wanted so much to teach them . . .

"But somebody else is doing it now; and that is well, too.

"Nearer and dearer duties content a man. And a dream, perhaps, is a vague thing after all.

"Only there is always that memory that it did actually begin to come true; that it might have come true, if . . .

"It is given to few men ever to realize their dreams, and perhaps that is the kinder way. . . ."

These were his dreams, all right, contained in the yellowing pages of his notes, the neat handwriting in his journals.

I read no further. I put the books back. But I would never again look at things in the same way. The morning's experience gave me an insight into my father's mind and heart which I might otherwise never have had.

For the first time I understood what had motivated him, what had sustained him. My own life would be shaped accordingly.

Back on my desk in my college room was a wooden cross carved for him by a West African chief. I had inherited it. Father had kept it always on his desk as a reminder of those thousands in the Sudan still waiting to hear the Word.

That cross was more than a symbol to me.

It was a call to action.

Six.

Minnehaha Falls

When I had stated publicly my intention to become a missionary at the time of my father's death, I was perfectly sincere. It had been an emotional decision, an almost instinctive reaction.

Yet the more I thought over my father's journals, the more certain I became that this was my life's purpose.

One point, however, still bothered me: How could I be a worthy missionary if I was still a mission field in myself? How could I win disciples if I was no real disciple?

"God has no grandchildren," I read one day, "only children." If that were true, then it meant that I could not inherit the faith of my parents. In some way, I had to make it my own.

It wasn't very hard for me to be a Christian while going to a Christian school. Sometimes, indeed, it was the line of least resistance. By praying a little louder and longer at our student prayer meetings, I maintained a shiny and convincing religious veneer.

But a sick heart lay beneath.

One summer when I was looking for a job, I heard that Trinity Church in Minneapolis needed secretarial help. I knew nothing about it except that it was a church with three pastors on the staff, near Minnehaha Falls. I applied and was hired.

In the church office I encountered an atmosphere of surprising happiness and spontaneity. Also, the first young people's meeting impressed me. There was something contagious in the enthusiasm of the teen-agers. Their Bibles were well-worn and marked; mine was in my room. In fact, I hadn't even bothered to unpack it.

The leader, Clifford Michelsen, worked the graveyard shift as a skilled laborer in a machine shop. He was given to expressing himself in the down-to-earth language of a workingman. He would challenge us with such statements as:

" 'He who loves not Christ *above* all, loves not Christ at all.' St. Augustine said that once. Does God really have the first place in your life?"

His words struck home. Would it really be possible—to love Christ more than my current boyfriend, my family, new clothes, ambitions? Myself?

Yet here was someone who did. Here were young people who practiced it. And look how radiantly happy they were! If only I could be one of them, laugh with them, pray with them . . .

I was living at the time only a few blocks from Minnehaha Falls. On long warm evenings I sat on the bench and pondered these questions as I gazed at the Statue of Hiawatha carrying Minnehaha across the stream.

Mother had often told me of the happy hours spent at Minnehaha with Father when they were engaged. But the quiet beauty of the scene, the peaceful sound of water gurgling over the smooth rocks, did nothing to relieve my inner burden—the ever-present load of despair which seemed to grow heavier day by day. It was hard to cope with because I could not grasp the cause of it all.

Everything seemed to torture me. The sermons I heard, the Bible studies to which I listened, seemed to point a finger of accusation at me. Words written almost two thousand years ago perfectly described my own condition: "Men shall be lovers of self. . . . holding a form of godliness, but having denied the power thereof. . . . But they shall proceed no further" (II Tim. 3:2,5,9).

I was miserable. But what could I do? It would have to be something tremendous if it was to relieve my distress. One day I thought I had the answer: I would rededicate myself. I'd go to Africa. By making this great sacrifice—so I assured myself in a flood of self-pitying tears—I would find joy and peace.

But even that decision didn't help.

It was a dry summer. With each succeeding day the trickle of the Falls grew smaller, and the diminishing trickle of well being in my heart dried up with it. For me, the sun did not shine, the birds did not sing. I was sick and I was blind.

In desperation I held out my empty hands to God: "Lord, I've had enough of this trying and striving to please you. The harder I try, the worse I feel. I see now, I do not love You above all things, nor can I ever—unless You take out this hard stone which is my heart and make it new. Make me one of your children so that I can sing, too, 'I know whom I have believed.' And show me the plan, purpose, and program you have for me in my life."

I cannot say that anything dramatic happened, anything spectacular. I can only say that God answered my prayer. For all at once something was changed deep down in my heart. There was a new glow and radiance in being alive.

Suddenly I grasped the meaning of the familiar words: "If any man is in Christ, he is a new creature: the old things are passed away; behold, they are become new" (II Cor. 5:17). With the blind man whom Jesus had healed I could say: "One thing I know, that, whereas I was blind, now I see" (John 9:25).

Reading my Bible became for me a thrilling experience. Verses leaped out at me. Words that had been dead letters before, were living forces now, springs offering refreshment: "The rivers of God are full of water."

One Saturday I went again to my refuge at Minnehaha Falls. After a heavy night's rain, the morning sun was dancing on the full cascading waters.

So this is what God could do! Instead of just a trickle, He could send torrents into a dry land, start springs in the valley, streams in the desert of a suffering heart.

Looking up, I saw a rainbow as the sunlight beamed through the droplets of spray. It called to my mind the rainbow that had encouraged Father and the other passengers on the *Zamzam*.

From then on my way was clear. God would lead me. I must take a step at a time. The next step was to finish college.

After completing my sophomore year at Luther Junior College in Wahoo in 1945, I went on to Augustana College in Rock Island, the same school both my parents had attended.

Since I had no money, I'd have to make my own way. I worked as a sales clerk in a bookstore and as a waitress in a café. I ironed shirts for seminarians at five cents a shirt; I sold men's long underwear across the counter at Montgomery-Ward.

There were not only financial ups-and-downs, but spiritual ones, too. One day I might be walking on clouds, and the next, plunged in the depths. Sometimes a nagging voice within me said: "Isn't it rather presumptuous of you to claim to be a child of God?"

One New Year's Eve I searched through my Bible for a word to quiet this voice. I found it finally in Isaiah 43:1, 3. The personal pronouns especially reassured me: "Fear not, for I have redeemed thee; I have called thee by thy name, thou art mine. . . . For I am the Lord thy God, the Holy One of Israel, thy Saviour." God had put into my hands a strong staff for my pilgrimage, not only for the new year but for all the years to come.

In June, 1947, I mounted the steps of the platform in the Augustana College gymnasium to receive my degree along with one hundred and thirty other seniors. It was a great day, a milestone on a road toward a clear goal: the Sudan.

As I sat on the hard chair in my cap and gown awaiting my turn, my thoughts went back to when my father had stood on this same platform and pleaded for the Sudan's needs. The church heard his plea. Three days later he was commissioned as its first missionary to that field.

I recalled some lines in my father's journal underscored in red and written when he was ordered to leave the Sudan and go to Tanganyika: "If we cannot remain in the Sudan, we leave it to God to find others to take the place that we might have occupied."

Now I thought: "Where are these others? Am I to be one of them? Will I follow in his footsteps?"

His time in the Sudan had been short, but he could never forget what he had seen and heard there. There was, for example, the king who welcomed my father with this greeting:

"For five years I have been looking up this road to see when the teacher of God should come. Today you have come."

A red-and-gold Koran that Father kept at the Homestead was a memento of that experience. Whenever visitors came, he would take it down from the bookshelf, carefully untie the beautifully tooled leather carrying case, and bring to view the holy book of Islam in its elaborate leather binding.

Then he would tell how he acquired it: After many days' trek through the mountains of northern Cameroun he arrived at the medieval capital of a kingdom called Rey Bouba. His carriers wanted to run away. They quaked with fear as they approached the high walls of the city, for they had heard many stories concerning Baba Rey, the cruel monarch who reigned as absolute master over his fifty thousand subjects.

My father informed the king he wished to visit him and give him the "God-palaver." The king received Father with kindness and invited him to stay in Rey Bouba for ten days as a royal guest.

Day after day the king sat fascinated as my father told him stories from the Bible, illustrating them with his picture roll.

When it came time for Father to leave, Baba Rey said to him:

"If you can get me these stories in my own language, in my own book, I will pay you a thousand francs."

My father smiled and shook his head.

"No," he said, "I will not accept the money"—and it was a solid sum in those days—"but I will exchange with you. If you give me a copy of your holy book, the Koran, I will see that you get a Bible in your language."

The king agreed. The book that played such an important part in our childhood was his gift. It was a great day whenever we children were allowed to touch it, to examine the elaborate title pages. Then it was put back in its place on the bookshelf.

Thinking now of that Koran, my heart beat faster.

When I had worked in Minneapolis in the summer of 1944, I talked to Missionary Gunderson, who had eventually followed Father into the Sudan. It was he who told me of Baba Rey's death and that the king's more liberal son now reigned.

"This means," Gunderson said, "that for the first time missionaries will be allowed to enter his kingdom, which hitherto has remained closed."

Perhaps this would be my opportunity. Perhaps one day I would stand in the presence of the king's son to make "God-palaver" with him, thus fulfilling the unfulfilled dream of my father.

It was to Missionary Gunderson that I sent my application after I graduated. I asked to be appointed to the Sudan Mission, working in Cameroun among the tribes which encircled Rey Bouba. But considerable preparation would lie ahead of me.

I enrolled for two terms in the missionary course at Lutheran Bible Institute. Besides the mission theory courses under the wisest of teachers, Dr. John Gronli, there were practical courses in dentistry, home nursing, and first aid. I also took a course in obstetrics at the local hospital.

I had dental work of my own to be done, for if I went to the Sudan, I would find no dentist within seven hundred miles. I had no notion how much it would cost.

Week after week I visited one of the best dentists in Minneapolis, until he pronounced that everything was in order. All that time I never had the courage to mention money. I trembled to think now of what his bill would be; it would come to at least two hundred dollars, I was sure. How could I pay it, when I didn't even have as much as twenty dollars? But I asked him for the bill anyway. He looked at me with a kindly smile and said:

"There is none. Please accept my services as my contribution toward your mission work."

I could hardly express my thanks.

Weeks went by and I heard nothing from Gunderson. Then—a morning's mail brought the letter from him. Oh, joyful day! The Sudan Mission Committee had acted favorably upon my application. But my jubilation was short-lived. The committee pointed out that before I left, I should have at least two thousand dollars in the bank.

I would need almost that sum to pay for my year's study in France. It was recommended that all missionaries have a French diploma in language proficiency before going to work in French Cameroun. I would also have to pay my transportation to the field. Then there was the matter of equipment—everything that I would need to set up a household in Africa. The mimeographed list which had been furnished me contained about three hundred items!

I was floored. Two thousand dollars! It was a fortune!

True, God had performed the miracle of getting me through college without incurring any debts—but now this!

It was the fall of 1948. I was employed by the First Lutheran Church in Rock Island as a parish worker. I got out my pencil and began to figure. With a great deal of scraping, I could put aside twenty-five dollars out of my monthly salary. But at that rate it would take me ten years to save up enough money. I was at the point of despair when a wise and kind friend gave me this advice: "Just take a step in faith. You will find that when you do, God meets you at the next step."

On the strength of this counsel, I wrote to a travel agency in

New York. After some correspondence I engaged passage on the S.S. *America* for February 17. The twenty-five-dollar deposit took the last cent I had.

I sent out a Christmas letter to my friends, telling them of my plans and inviting them to my commissioning service at First Lutheran Church on January 23.

Then I saw what God can do. One day Pastor William Berg asked me for a list of the items I'd need. I had no idea why he wanted it. That afternoon I saw he had tacked it on the bulletin board of the parish hall where his members could hardly miss it. When I looked the list over I was somewhat overwhelmed: kerosene lamps; tools; flat irons; camping equipment; water filter; coffee grinder; food chopper with butter knife for making peanut butter; Christmas decorations; kitchenware; dishes; linen. At the bottom, in his own handwriting, Pastor Berg had appended a note suggesting that perhaps the members of the congregation might find some of these things at home.

Then everything happened at once. As I passed through the church basement, I saw men busily making wooden boxes. When next I saw them packing the boxes with miscellaneous items, I knew what was going on.

Ex-service students at Augustana College and Seminary had donated their army blankets, a camp cot, and a sleeping bag. There were enough pots and pans to set up a kitchen unit for a small army. By this time I was finding it hard to keep my feet on the ground, especially since I was already lightheaded from my typhus shots and smallpox vaccination.

A young woman reporter on the local paper, believing I would make a good story for her weekly feature, "Career Girl," asked me for an interview. After recounting the adventures of the "vivacious, titian-haired missionary, twenty-two years of age," she concluded: "Here is one field, girls, that we can guarantee is not overcrowded."

Although I was almost overburdened with equipment, I still had not solved the problem of the money. Just as I was really starting to worry, that, too, began coming in, mainly in small gifts. What touched me was that the larger gifts always came from those who could least afford it. A check for twenty-five dollars, for example, had been given by one of the poorest widows in the congregation, who lived on a small pension. Another twenty-five dollars had come from a family with four children, living without salary while the father took special training for the mission field.

I shall never forget the letter from a little boy in a reform school whose home I had visited while a parish worker. (He was only eight and his offense was stealing a car.) He wrote: "Dear Miss Hult, I wish you a Happy New Year when you go on your trip. I am giving you this gift. I hope it will help you as you go to Africa. God bless you." Fastened to the letter with Scotch tape was a fifty-cent piece.

This would be my last Christmas in the States for some time. I decided to spend it with relatives at Maplehurst, the home of my mother's parents at Geneseo.

One morning my aunt told me of a black trunk which Mother had stored in one of the upstairs bedrooms. Perhaps, she said, I would find something there that I might need for Africa. I sat down on the floor beside it and pushed open the catch.

When I looked inside I felt a lump in my throat. I recognized the contents as Father's personal effects found in his hotel room at Dar es Salaam. Among them were the last letters from his family, his Bible, his hymnal, and even an egg cup and napkin ring carved out of ebony which someone must have given him. And here was his treasured walking stick! Kind Pastor Melander had brought this trunk back from Africa with him.

Next, I came on a knee-length black coat something like a Prince Albert. Of course! That was Father's Prästock, the garment which Swedish pastors used to wear. He had worn it at so many important occasions in his life: when he was ordained; when he was commissioned as a missionary to the Sudan; when he was married; when each of his children was baptized. I could see him in it now, standing in the pulpit of the little country churches where he served as temporary pastor during those long years of exile from Africa. Tears started to my eyes.

I looked at it long. It was in fine condition, but who would ever wear it? The woolen material was priceless. And then I had an idea. I could make a jacket out of it and wear it at my commissioning service. It would be a precious symbol for me.

In late January six of my brothers and sisters came to be present at the cermony: Veda from Omaha, where she was in nurse's training; Eunie from Lindsborg, where she was a junior at Bethany College; Carl and Martha from Luther College in Wahoo; Gus from Geneseo, where he lived with relatives; John and his wife, Louise—they were married while he was still a senior at Washington University Medical School—from St. Louis. Only Mother, Mary, David, and Paul were not present.

Pastor Berg read a greeting from Mother in Bolivia:

"My heart is filled with thanksgiving to God that He has called Ingrid to go to the Sudan with the good news of redemption.

"As you know, my husband and I have prayed for the people there for many years. Therefore, it gives me the greatest joy a Christian mother can know when this prayer is to be answered in one of our own children. And I know there is rejoicing in heaven."

Those next days were to me "miracle days," for truly showers came from heaven. I had paid for my ticket to France, and already I had seventeen hundred dollars in my bank account. My trunks and boxes were packed with far more than the three hundred items listed.

The last Sunday in my home church I remarked to the congregation:

"I feel as though I am being let down into a pit. I am so glad to know that you folks at home will be holding the ropes in prayer."

The next day my train pulled out of the Rock Island station.

Moved to the depths of my heart, I watched as that faithful group who had come down to see me off, receded into the distance. Very real to me was a long, long rope being unwound with each mile the train sped on its way.

The end of that rope was secure.

On my way east I stopped in Philadelphia to visit my oldest brother Paul, Ann, his wife, and their little curly-headed Betsy. Paul was now a senior at Temple University.

He looked at me wistfully and said:

"I'm glad you can go to Africa, Ingrid. In fact, I'm envious of you and I wish I were going too." Then he added: "But I am not entirely happy that you are going alone. I wish you had a husband."

He became slightly impatient when I told him that I must be obedient and go to France and even to Africa without one.

"But do you expect that God is going to drop you a husband down out of heaven?" he asked.

I gently reminded him of Mother's advice to her daughters: "Far better to be not married, than married to the wrong man."

Paul's comment brought to mind a conversation with Father back at the Homestead.

On warm Sundays Father would set up his camp chair in the yard under the great oak tree, and one by one, we children each took turns sitting on the little African stool at his side.

One Sunday Father's lesson was about the virgin birth. He used the occasion to explain to me the "facts of life" or rather the miracle of life. I must have been about ten years old. I listened thankfully and quietly as my frank questions were answered with equal frankness.

And then Father said:

"Ingrid, you are not too young to begin praying for the one who will be your life partner."

I never forgot that advice. As an adolescent, as a college student, I had followed it. During the war years I had felt at times a real urgency in my prayers. Perhaps this partner of mine was on some distant battlefield, in great danger, and I prayed that God would protect him while I waited for him.

Of course, there were friendships with young men who embodied my ideals. But always on the threshold of a deeper friendship, I would hear an inner voice saying:

"No, Ingrid, this is not the one for whom you have prayed. This is not the partner for you."

Now I began to wonder if I would ever find him. I was already twenty-two and most of my girl friends were engaged, many of them married.

My overwhelming emotion as the gangplank of the huge S.S. *America* was drawn up at Pier 61 on North River, Thursday afternoon, February 17, 1949, was one of utter loneliness. The band was playing. People waved from the pier. Among them I spotted a head of dark brown curly hair. Vivacious Ann with little Betsy had come to New York to see me off. But I could not catch her eye.

The ship began to move. This was the moment, the goal of long years of preparation. But I knew no one on board—only the number of my tourist-class cabin. I would find it, hide myself, and weep.

I was searching for it down the long corridors when a smartly uniformed bellboy came by, paging someone as he rang his little bell.

Why, he was calling my name! I followed him and touched his sleeve. He looked at me for a moment and then said:

"Who are you, anyway? A movie actress, or somep'n? I got some mail for you—and I *do* mean some!" His arms were full of letters. "And there's more in the purser's office!"

He still looked at me curiously until I explained:

"I'm only a missionary on my way to Paris, bound eventually for Africa. Perhaps it's because today's my birthday that all these people have written. I'd quite forgotten in the excitement of sailing."

I cried when I saw all the mail. But these were tears of happiness. The letter that encouraged me most was from my own Pastor Berg, who wrote:

"Happy Birthday! And I have the feeling that this is the finest and happiest birthday of your life. And say—if you could fully realize how many prayers are reaching the Throne of Grace in your behalf today—and how fervent they are—your joy would be as boundless as the ocean wide upon which you sail.

"Your life has been gloriously full and fruitful. But the best is yet ahead: adventure for Christ and for souls, beyond your fondest dreams and expectations.

"Here's a word for you from last Sunday's text: You recall the parable of the Laborers and the Hours. The first workers bargained with the householder in Matthew 20:2. But the next ones trusted him when he said, *'Go . . . and whatsoever is right I will give you.'* You trust—He will provide."

Seven.

Paris and a Prince

Paris to me meant dim, winding stairways where strange odors met us; dark rooms with red curtains, red bedspreads, sometimes even red wallpaper. I received these first vivid impressions while I was room hunting with some American friends.

Most of this room hunting was done in the Latin Quarter with its narrow sidewalks, cobblestone streets, and gray buildings. It was like a scene from a Victor Hugo novel. I saw little boys walking home from school with berets, wooden shoes, and knapsacks on their backs.

Before I left the States a friend had told me there are three qualities essential to every new missionary. The first: adaptability. The second, like unto the first: adaptability. And the third, a combination of the first two: adaptability. I would need all these qualities in the months ahead.

The last address on our list was just a stone's throw from the Luxembourg Gardens. A woman doctor, Mlle. Tisserand, lived there.

The room, on the ground floor, was lighter than any I had seen. A glass door opened onto a small garden, where at noon a bit of sunshine found its way in over the high walls. The price was good too, only three thousand francs a month (about ten dollars). If I wished, she said, I could take my meals with her.

I went into a huddle with my friends, and we decided this would be the ideal room. It was only a short distance to school. I paid down the first month's rent. My friends left, agreeing to meet me later.

I took a better look at my lodgings. It was a miniature "hall of mirrors": no less than five in this one room—one over the fireplace, one over my bed, a full-length dressing mirror, as well as two on the wardrobe doors. And the bed was a genuine Louis Philippe.

Dr. Tisserand and I soon became good friends. She did research work on heredity and also lectured at the Sorbonne. Through her I learned to appreciate the French mind, which values clarity and precision above all. Someone has said: "That which is not clear is not French." I remember reading Albert Schweitzer's comparison of the language to German. "When I speak French," he said, "I have the impression of walking through a beautiful garden with everything in perfect order. But when I speak German, I am walking through a deep forest."

As I strolled through the streets of Paris, I observed that the expression of individuality seemed to be of prime importance. I understood what André Siegfried meant when he wrote: "Two Frenchmen, two political parties." A French student once said to me: "You Americans are given much freedom as children. By the time you are twenty, you are quite willing to conform. We must as children conform to a strict pattern in our family life. By twenty we are revolutionaries."

I was never lonely. There were almost a hundred missionaries from many different countries studying in Paris to prepare for work in French-speaking Africa and in Madagascar. Our fellowship in Christ quickly surmounted denominational and national barriers.

One of the missionaries was a girl from Fergus Falls, Min-

nesota, named Helen Arnseth. Helen was preparing to go out to
Madagascar as a teacher. As we got better acquainted, I came to
call her "Let's-have-a-party-Arnseth." Whenever we met a group
in our French courses or at one of the student restaurants, she
would turn to me and say: "Let's have a party and invite them
over."

What a missionary field Paris seemed to offer! Here were sixty
thousand students at the Sorbonne from many nationalities and
walks of life and without much Christian fellowship among them.

I was intrigued for a time by the possibilities of work to be
done right around me and even began to talk to others about my
plans. Then Dawson Trotman, founder of The Navigators, came
to Paris. He shared my enthusiasm over the challenge to be
met here. But he also made it clear to me that this was no work
for a young girl, since it might lead to too many difficult and
embarrassing situations. Six weeks later he sent a man to Paris to
begin the work which I had in mind. Meanwhile, I concentrated
all my energies once more on preparing for Africa.

It was a happy summer. But then one afternoon, returning
from classes, I found on the hall table a letter from Eunie. The
first few lines shattered my tranquillity. She was writing to tell me
that Gus, now fifteen, had suffered a serious injury.

It had been a foolish-boy accident. Gus and some friends were
returning by car from a youth meeting in a town near Genesco. It
was a warm summer evening. Gus sat on the right fender, one
friend on the left, while another friend, Bob, drove home. At one
point Bob had to swerve out of the path of an oncoming car.
Bob's line of vision was cut off and he couldn't see how close he
was to a parked car on the right. His right front wheel scraped
against it and Gus's foot was crushed in between.

Gus looked down and saw his right foot dangling, connected to
his leg only by the tendons and a bit of flesh. His first reaction
was "How could this possibly happen to me?" He told his friends
to put him in the back seat and drive quickly to the police station.

From there he was rushed to the hospital, where the battle to save his foot began.

A bone surgeon was called in. Since the artery had not been severed, he decided not to amputate immediately. He wanted to give it every chance—although his better judgment told him there was scarcely a chance in a thousand that the foot could be saved.

News of the accident spread quickly among our friends and fellow church members. Eunie said there were many who prayed. Two days later there was the faintest sign of life in the foot. It was warm; circulation had begun. "A miracle," the surgeon said, "but there's still a long ordeal ahead. A series of operations will be required, plus long periods in the hospital, and constant nursing care."

I put the letter down and began to pace the floor.

How like Eunie, I thought, not to let me know until Gus was out of danger!

But those medical bills! They would amount to hundreds—if not thousands—of dollars. Did I have the right to go on with my missionary career while my loyal brothers and sisters bore this burden?

I did not see how, in all conscience, I could. But what should I do? Go back to the States and find a job in order to help with my fair share?

That would mean a long delay in taking up the work to which I had been called. I would have to start all over again, and then where would I get the money? The trip home and back would take all that was left of my savings.

And what about those who had expressed their faith in me by contributing to the cost of my training? How would they feel when they saw me turn up again at home?

I continued my pacing. I had to think this out carefully. There was no easy solution.

Then my heart turned to Mother in Bolivia. She must be thinking the same thoughts, facing the same dilemma.

Should she come home? Her term of four years was not yet half over. She had made a place for herself at the orphanage, where she was badly needed. I knew she would decide only after she had heard from each of her children.

Veda expressed the sentiments of all of us when she wrote to Mother soon afterward:

"I definitely feel that if your health is good, you should stay on for two more years in Bolivia. You will not need to come back on account of any of your children. I say this not because it wouldn't mean a lot to us to have you here, but because it would mean a lot more to those whom you serve, for you to stay."

In this spirit I made up my mind to continue my studies in Paris. We all tried to help financially as best we could. The experience served to knit us closer together as a family.

For Gus it became a spiritual turning point. Up until the time of the accident he had shown promise as an athlete and intended to make baseball his career. One of my mother's brothers, who had been a big league player, encouraged him. Now Gus's hopes were dashed. He would have to look in a new direction.

Gus wrote:

"I know that God has another plan for my life and I pray that He will show it to me."

About Christmas time I received a letter from Germany. It was from a young pastor named Walter Trobisch, who had been present at my commissioning service in Rock Island while he was studying at Augustana Seminary on an exchange program. On that occasion he had asked that his name be put on the mailing list for my newsletter. That's how he knew my address.

He was back in Germany, serving as assistant pastor at a church in Ludwigshafen. He said he would like very much to have me speak to his young people's group before I left for Africa. He stated that while he was in America, he had occasionally been asked to speak and had always used the opportunity to try to build a bridge of forgiveness and understanding to heal the wounds of the war. He felt that if I could come, we would do the same thing together in Germany.

I wasted no time in replying. I told him that it was quite out of the question for me even to consider the trip.

But one evening in February as I was sitting in my French geography class, I glanced casually at my map of Europe. I happened to notice that Ludwigshafen was not far from the French border. We would be having a five-day holiday for Mardi Gras. I don't know how to explain it, for it sounds so foolish, but suddenly I had to go to Germany. I sent a telegram; the reply came quickly: "WELCOME!"

It was a strange feeling to be getting off the Paris train at Ludwigshafen, a gray, dismal, industrial city. I kept asking myself, "What am I doing here? What would Mother think?" But there was no turning back. There he was waiting for me, wearing a motorcycle suit designed to keep out both wind and rain. The suit didn't exactly flatter him, I thought.

Walter explained casually that he was in a hurry, since he had to leave immediately for a youth meeting. But a friend would take me to the pastor's home where I would be staying. This offhand reception did little to warm my feelings toward him. His friend, the music director of the church, took me on the street car to Pastor Kreiselmaier's house.

The minute I entered the door, I felt better. Mrs. Kreiselmaier was as kind to me as if I were her daughter.

I did not see him again until Sunday evening, when we attended a youth rally at which Walter and I both spoke. We were delighted by the response of the German young people. We sensed an unexpected blessing on our teamwork. What did it mean? At the same time our relationship was very impersonal. All our conversations were strictly business.

The next day Walter asked me if I were afraid to ride with him on his motorcycle. I could hardly refuse, although I'd never been

on a motorcycle in my life, let alone in the month of February
when it was cold and wet.

"Good!" he said. "Then I'd like to show you the work of the
Volksmission here. But it'll mean a thirty-mile ride on the back of
my machine. Can you take it?"

I nodded stoically.

Mrs. Kreiselmaier searched her daughter's closets for all the
warm clothing she could find.

Bundled in sweaters, two jackets, ski pants, overshoes, scarves,
and even a helmet, I took my place—not on a dashing white
steed but on the back saddle of Walter's powerful Horex.

I was quietly terrified. Once we were out on the highway, I
began to relax, then actually to enjoy myself. It was a new experience for me, traveling through the quaint wine villages of the
Palatinate. But we had not gone far when it began to rain. It was
worse than rain, in fact—half rain, half sleet. There was not
much romance left now. More than once the motorcycle slipped
and we fell in the mud. But I didn't say anything, nor was I ready
to give up.

At last we arrived at the village of Annweiler. We knocked at
the door of the parsonage. The pastor's wife exclaimed in surprise
when she saw on her doorstep not one, but two, soaked and
shivering wayfarers.

"Come in quickly," she said. "Get those wet clothes off. Sit by
the fire and I'll bring you some hot water in which to soak your
feet."

What a picture we made as we sat drinking hot coffee, the
same warm blanket draped about our shoulders, and soaking our
feet together in the same basin! To me it was embarrassing, to say
the least. But Walter appeared to be enjoying it all immensely. He
looked at me with a twinkle in his eyes and said:

"What would your friends say if they could see you right
now?"

Just at this moment we heard the town crier proclaim an evangelistic service to be held the same evening in the village church.

Sitting with our feet in the basin, Walter told me that since the Protestant church had been completely destroyed by bombing raids, the meeting would be held in the Catholic church. Those on the program would include a woman physician, a farmer, a factory worker, and a high school teacher. I would give a greeting from America.

I shall never forget that evening.

The church was a large one, with lofty ceilings. It was so cold that we kept on our coats even while we spoke.

The audience listened attentively to each message. And then it was Walter's turn. Clad in his rubberized motorcycle suit, he related the story of his visit to America. I didn't understand what he was saying, for it was all in German, but I could not avert my gaze from him.

And then it came to me—that strong Inner Voice:

"Ingrid, you have been praying all these years for the one who is right to be your life partner. This is he."

I gasped. My reaction must have been almost audible. I was shocked and thought: "No! Why, he isn't my ideal at all."

Walter had a position as a youth pastor here. I was called to Africa. How could our careers ever fit together?

The service ended. It was decided that instead of driving back the thirty miles in the cold winter night, we would wait until morning.

I was invited to stay at the pastor's home. His wife, who could speak English, offered me cocoa and cakes before I retired. Their house was being repaired, and I asked about it. Only then did she tell me in a quiet voice of the night their home had been bombed. In the very room in which we sat, their only daughter had been killed. No more was said, but I began to realize the miracle that had been wrought that they could now receive me with such grace.

I didn't sleep much. All these impressions were too great.

On the way back to Ludwigshafen the next morning, we exchanged only polite, impersonal remarks. In another day I'd be leaving for Paris. Walter said he'd come early in the afternoon to visit before preparing together for a youth meeting in the evening.

"At last!" I thought. "Perhaps the barriers between us will be broken down." But he did not come—not at one o'clock, nor at two o'clock, nor even at three. It was four-thirty when he finally appeared. His only explanation was that he thought I needed rest and that it would also give him a good chance to catch up on his correspondence. I was speechless with fury.

"What's the matter, Ingrid?" Walter asked, perplexed. "I can feel that something is bothering you. You must share it with me or else there will be no blessing on our meeting tonight."

So I poured out everything that was on my mind. I accused him of using me to further his own interests. Oh, he was kind enough to me, I said, but in the way one would be kind to a little prize dog. This cold indifference—what did it mean? Why had I come at all? Why hadn't I stayed in Paris where I belonged?

Walter looked at me in amazement. He first tried to explain his attitude of indifference. He was sure, he said, that he ought to remain single for some years yet, in order to have his hands free for the Lord's work alone.

Then he continued:

"I know of no girl in whom I could be more interested than you, but I would break into your life, which is so well-organized and well-ordered, like a bull in a chinashop."

It was time for the evening meal and the youth meeting.

The next day he took me to the train. We agreed to be quiet before God until He showed the next step.

Upon my return to Paris I found letters from home awaiting me. I was delighted to learn that Gus was making good progress. The second operation on his foot, which included a bone graft, had been successful. He could get around on crutches.

Another letter brought the news that Eunie, four years younger than I, would soon be married. Her prospective husband was Vincent Will, who had been with the army in Italy and in North Africa. I had met Vince at Luther Academy. He was strong and straightforward, a gifted musician and artist. As a soldier in Casablanca, he had sensed God's call through contacts with French and American missionaries. Now he was training to be a missionary to Moslems.

Before I left the States, Eunie had confided that they were engaged. I looked at her left hand. There was no diamond.

"Vince had saved the money for it and we were going to pick it out together," she explained. "Then we heard that funds were needed immediately for a mission project in Africa. So my ring went into the collection plate. Neither of us has regretted it."

Their wedding would follow the same pattern. Instead of an expensive formal ceremony, they planned to be married in street clothes at the closing session of the Youth Conference at Wahoo.

"God first, others second, and ourselves last. That would be the motto of their life together," I thought after I had read the letter.

How I wished I could be present for their great day!

In June I passed the examination for the coveted *Diplôme Supérieur,* which entitled me to teach at a French school in Cameroun. After this ordeal I felt the need of a vacation before going on to Africa.

My thoughts turned to Germany. Walter found a room for me with the widow of a German painter in the Odenwald. The quiet beauty of the countryside reminded me of the Ozarks. Every Monday, when he was free from his pastoral duties fifty miles away at Ludwigshafen, my prince on the motorcycle would come to visit me.

On one of his visits Walter told me the story of his life. He was born in Leipzig, the largest city in East Germany outside of Berlin, where his parents were both teachers. There he spent a happy and uneventful childhood together with his younger sister and brother. At the age of eighteen he was drafted into Hitler's army. Soon he found himself in the infantry, marching over the plains of Russia.

He was not cut out to be a soldier. It was a favorite saying of his mother that "from the moment Walter was drafted, Germany began to lose the war."

Walter was twice wounded in Russia, first in the Battle of Stalingrad and then in the Ukraine, each time just before the German army was surrounded. The second time he was tossed onto the last truck carrying the wounded back to safety. A hospital train took him to Vienna.

While recuperating from his injuries, he was given permission by a Christian doctor to attend day classes at the university. He began to study for the ministry, an unpopular thing to do while Hitler was still in power. God's protecting hand obliged him to take this step.

When he recovered, he was sent back to the front. Finally, in April, 1945, he was captured near Nürnberg in Bavaria by an American Negro soldier. This was the first Negro he had ever seen. A few days later the war in Europe ended. Because he could prove that he had never been a member of the Nazi party, Walter was released from P.O.W. camp within three weeks. By the end of May he was able to start home. No trains were running. Bridges had been blown up. He covered the two hundred miles on foot in little more than a week.

He returned safely after his grim experiences to find an empty place in the family circle. His only sister, Herta, eighteen years old, had died of diphtheria in a Hitler work camp for girls. The apartment had been badly damaged by bombs. But Walter and the three remaining members of the family had no time to grieve. They had their hands full, fighting to survive the cold and starvation.

In July, 1945, the American troops that had occupied Leipzig withdrew, and the Russians took over. The city was cut off from the rest of the free world. Walter enrolled in the University of Leipzig and continued his studies.

After a few months he was asked to represent the young people of the Protestant church on the Leipzig youth council, which included, besides himself, a Catholic and ten Communists. Every time he left home, his mother wondered whether she would see him again. One morning he was told secretly that the council held a meeting the night before without him. His life was in danger.

The next morning his mother sewed some paper money into the seams of his shirt. He packed a few necessities in a knapsack and set out. At the border he was befriended by a farmer. He remained for a time, pretending to work in the fields right under the Russian watchtowers. He noticed that every day at noon, the guards left their posts to go into a restaurant. One day he waited for this moment to come, then walked boldly through the Iron Curtain in broad daylight.

Walter had barely enough money to buy a train ticket to Heidelberg. He arrived there penniless. But a friend helped him out and made it possible for him to enroll at the university to finish his studies. He had just one year left. It was on the university's recommendation that he had received the year's scholarship at Augustana Seminary where we met for the first time.

During my stay in the Odenwald Walter showed me, one afternoon, an entry he had made in his notebook when he was thirteen. He had written down the reasons for his wanting to become a missionary to Africa. I was astonished. For the first time I felt our paths might merge. Then, closing the notebook, he said abruptly that he still felt that his call was to continue to work as a youth pastor in Germany. And I was just as certain that my call was to go to Africa. Once more we were not sure whether God wanted our lives to be blended into one.

In this time of confusion we took Walter's friend, Pastor Fuchs, into our confidence. We confessed our doubts as to how our lives might fit together in the future.

"A Christian," he answered simply, "is one who can wait."

And so, more or less reconciled to waiting, we said good-by. I returned to Paris and packed my trunks for Africa. Our love was strong and deep, but we did not know when, where—or even if—we would ever meet again.

Eight.

"Sanoo! Sanoo!"*

On board S.S. *Banfora*, September 11, 1950

Dear Walter,

Here I am, bound for Africa at last.

Our ship just slipped gracefully out of the ancient harbor of Marseilles into the calm waters of the Mediterranean. The weather is perfect. I found a quiet spot up on deck, hidden behind a pile of ropes, where I can watch the sea and write to you.

I have just been reading my father's journal, which I brought with me. This is an entry he wrote back in 1919, when he was sailing to Africa for the first time: "The one overwhelming experience at sea is for me the note of eternity . . . For a son of the prairies, the sea is never monotonous . . . It's most impressive to see the officers take the position of the ship again and again, and to find that over a pathless expanse we have not erred from our way."

The strong promise for this day I found in Psalm 18: "God . . . girdeth me with strength. . . ."

I need it, for I am very lonesome. I'm the only American on

* This chapter is composed of excerpts from correspondence between Walter and me over a two-year period.

board. Most of the other passengers are French administrators who, with their wives and children, are on their way to some post in Africa. They are gay, evidently determined to make the most of their last fourteen days in a French atmosphere.

Before we sailed, I had a chance to go to Rome. There I stood one evening on the Appian Way, the same road over which the Apostle Paul had walked before he went to the Eternal City to die. What a moment! It was as if I could hear him speak to me those last words he wrote in his prison cell as he handed the torch to his young disciple Timothy: "I charge thee in the sight of God, and of Christ Jesus. . . . fulfil thy ministry" (II Tim. 4:1, 5).

Dakar, September 18

Today we landed in Dakar right on the big hump of West Africa.

I like the colors—the dark green palms contrasting with brown roofs and cream-colored buildings and the almost red earth. Everything one reads of Africa is true: the misery, the dirt, the smells. There's something also that one doesn't read about—a sort of resignation and indifference—no complaining, or nothing of desperation, just a sort of apathy.

. . . As for ourselves, while it is hard for both of us, I wouldn't want it any other way between us than it is now. It's right to have a sort of delightful uncertainty about the future. God has been unique in His methods of bringing us together. I shall be happy to have each day filled with work for Him. You will be very busy too, and that will give a meaning to our separation. I agree with what you said in your last letter: "Let's both work as if there would be no love, and love as if there would be no work."

At sea, September 23

This is the last night at sea. Tomorrow we shall be in Douala! My heart is filled with mingled emotions—to think that I am now so close to the land to which God has called me.

Last night I dreamed of my father. He was so very real. You

were there too, and we all three talked together. Even after I woke up, his presence lingered, so that it was hard to persuade myself it had been a dream. I don't know why God is so good to me, to have given me such a heritage as I had in my home—such faith and love and understanding. And now to have the great gift of your heart's confidence as well. I can't help but think of the future even though it's nebulous. Is that wrong?

Douala, September 25

Yesterday we sailed by the majestic Mount Cameroun caught in the rays of the afternoon sun and landed quietly in the Douala harbor about four o'clock. The pier was crowded with people waiting to welcome the passengers.

Never in my life have I felt more alone. I knew that none of our missionaries would be here, for our closest station is a thousand miles inland. I was afraid of all that was ahead, of my inability to face it. I wanted to run back to my cabin and hide.

But then I heard someone calling my name. It was Mr. Monnier, a Swiss, who meets arriving missionaries. In a few minutes he had my baggage off the boat and was escorting me to my room in the old mission house.

Regretfully, Mr. Monnier excused himself; he and his wife had a dinner invitation. They hoped I wouldn't mind being left alone on my first evening ashore. I smiled bravely and said of course I wouldn't. So there I was by myself in a gray, uninviting room, with the African night coming on. From without, I heard the street cries. Again I was overwhelmed by this heavy feeling of being alone—all alone. I went out and walked up and down the old wooden veranda, listening to the strange new sounds, afraid even of the shadows.

But all of a sudden I knew I was not alone. Jesus was very near. The heavy weight lifted from my heart. I could spend those first hours in Africa with Him and even sing the praises of Psalm 103.

Ludwigshafen, October 8

Dear Ingrid,

It's been a great adventure to be with you. But I think it will be a still greater adventure to let you go for obedience' sake and to go with you through this hard school of believing without seeing.

Faith is a risk on God. Life is a risk on God. Love is a risk on God. . . . All that we now experience will be used by the Lord in some way. Nothing will be in vain. The long darkness we endure will become illuminating lightnings; the separation will become a finding-again, more beautiful than ever. The salt will come into our testimony through the period we have to live through now—the period of separation, of certain uncertainty, of a blind flight in a definite direction.

Douala, October 15

Thanks for every word. I certainly never felt like a jungle queen until you addressed me that way in one of your letters. When I crawled into bed under the mosquito net, I pretended it was a canopy over a throne. I could look out my window and see the gorgeous tropical vegetation in the light of a full moon. What more could I want, except a prince to share such beauty?

It is raining—as it has done almost every hour since my arrival. Douala is the second rainiest city in the world, I'm told, and this is the height of the rainy season.

It is also my first experience with a tropical downpour. This is no gentle pitter-patter, but an unremitting deluge in sheets. When the rain lets up, it is warm, so that it is somewhat like living in a hothouse. There is no escape from it. The sheets on my bed are always clammy. Mold gathers on my shoes. Everything has a musty, tropical smell.

And then just when my spirits have hit bottom, I receive word from Mr. Okland, one of our missionaries who's coming down in the mission truck to meet me in Yaounde, the capital of Cameroun, that because of the heavy rains he won't be able to get through until the end of October.

And so I wait—for the ship from America which is to bring my baggage and for the railroad to be repaired after another landslide. Mr. Monnier likes to tease me. This morning at breakfast he said: "Hurry up and get ready, Ingrid. Your train is leaving next month." I guess Pastor Fuchs is right: "A Christian is one who can wait."

The week began with a wonderful promise: "I . . . will do better unto you than at your beginnings: and ye shall know that I am the Lord" (Ezek. 36:11). I am full of expectation. To go with a promise in the heart through the fog (or through the rain) that is life.

Douala, October 20

I must learn many lessons in adjustment these days of waiting. . . . Often I look at the picture of you on your motorcycle which always says to me, "Be happy, as I . . ."

At the moment I'm typing out a large packet of notes written by my father as he was exploring the territory in northern Cameroun. They are a day-to-day account of his experiences and impressions which make me all the more eager to see that country for myself. . . .

I've just had a most exciting experience. Here I was typing away when I came suddenly upon an entry written by my mother in 1923, describing their stay in Douala at the Old Basel Mission House. This is the very place where I am staying. This discovery has given me an entirely different perspective. Now I feel at home.

Yaounde, October 28

At last, at last, I'm on the way! The train is rolling slowly but steadily toward Yaounde, which is two hundred miles from Douala. But beyond Yaounde there's still another eight hundred miles to be covered by truck before I reach Poli where I'm to be stationed.

Right now we're passing through the virgin forest—beautiful, yet frightening at the same time. I'm beginning to understand that Africa is like an inverted saucer; all around the rim are the low-altitude coastal areas; the higher plateaus are toward the center. Right now we're slowly climbing the Yaounde plateau.

Garoua-Boulai, November 6

Greetings from the first station of the Sudan Mission I have encountered on the way upcountry! Last Saturday afternoon, after riding for two days in the Dodge pickup truck over muddy and bumpy roads, we came to a little sign which said: "Mission Protestante." Believe me it was a welcome sight, for every bone and muscle was sore from the bouncing around.

Looking up the hill, I saw the two simple missionary homes and a cluster of native huts. A minute later our truck was surrounded by the ten children of missionaries who attend school here, the houseparents and teacher. There was a gala dinner that evening. On my place card it said: "Welcome to our family—Psalm 67."

The house in which I'm staying is built of dried mud with a straw roof. It has mud floors covered with bamboo mats. But the walls are whitewashed and the missionaries have added touches which make it quite homelike. We have a wonderful bathtub, made by sawing a metal oil drum in half, and then painting it with white enamel. The other half, set up on a base made from a packing box, serves as the kitchen sink.

On Sunday I gave my first greeting to the native church. The little grass-roofed chapel was filled to overflowing. I told them about my father, how he had traveled through this area, then had wanted to come back, but was never able to do so. Then I told them why I was here—how, when he died, I knew I had to carry on where he left off and now I could begin.

Garoua-Boulai, November 15

Laura Burton, a nurse here at the station, has been sharing her room with me.

Last night we couldn't get to sleep. There was an indescribable feeling in the air of something evil. After a while we heard crying and shouting in the village half a mile away.

A few minutes later somebody pounded on our door. Two men wanted Laura to examine a man they thought was dead. She snatched her medicine bag and went with them. There, so she told me later, she found people crying, shouting, screaming.

A young fellow, who appeared to be in the best of health, had suddenly dropped dead. Word went round that he had been killed by an evil spirit. It was generally assumed that someone had displeased the spirit. Now they've sent for the witchdoctor. The missionaries fear that a series of other deaths will result.

This was my first encounter with the fearsome aspect of the African night. The presence and power of evil was so palpable it was almost choking. Yet it was elusive—not an enemy that one could strike at—and for that reason all the more terrifying.

Oh, how we feel the need of prayer, to have the courage and faith to stand firm. We told ourselves that darkness has never yet put out a light, but that the greater the darkness, the brighter the light shines.

It's sobering to be here. Now that I see the conditions under which the missionaries work, and am aware of the size of the area they have to cover, I'm overwhelmed. It's all so different from what I saw in southern Cameroun where they've had a chance to hear the Word now for two or three generations.

Gone, too, is much of the exotic tropical beauty that one sees on the coast—no more romantic palms and breath-taking views. Rather the country has a barren look. More than ever it will be necessary to keep a spirit of beauty and purity in the heart, for there is little of it to be found outside. That, too, is why your letters and those from my family mean so much.

With the coming of daylight the sinister feeling disappeared. Nevertheless I was greatly relieved when I caught sight of Reubin Johnson, the missionary at Poli, who had come to get me in his pickup truck.

Poli, November 16

This is a continuation of my last letter. The rest of the drive was magnificent, especially when we crossed the mountain range just after Ngaoundere.

Every hill, every village we passed, had a special meaning for me, because we were going over the same route that my father had traveled. In following his path I was experiencing something of the same thrill that he told us he had felt when, on his last trip upcountry, he followed in Livingstone's footsteps.

You should have seen the Africans dance for joy when the truck drove into the station at Poli. The first to greet me was Samuel, a Sara. (This was the tribe to which my father had felt such a strong call. Remember?)

He kept saying, *"Sanoo! Sanoo!"* which in Fulani is both the greeting and the expression of thankfulness for my safe arrival. Harriet Stovner, who was a student in Paris at the same time I was, came running to greet me and I felt at home immediately. She will be my co-worker here.

We're learning to keep house, African style. Water must be carried up from the river, and boiled and filtered before we can use it. Wood is our fuel, but a boy must go a couple of miles into the forest to fetch it and then he must carry it home on his head. Kerosene lamps must be cleaned and filled, mosquito nets put up, not to mention dozens of other duties which are not needed back home.

Poli, January 10, 1951

Now I would like to ask you a question. Do you think it is really true that "everything that is separated shall meet again"? I am experiencing a suffering new to me—this pain of separation —and at times it becomes a heavy ache in my heart.

I can understand so well how my father must have felt when for long months he received no word from Mother because her letters were lost.

But there is a joy in even this sorrow. It's the joy of becoming empty like an open hand which holds nothing but can only wait until something will be put into it. It is the joy of being no longer self-sufficient, but out of the whole heart, weak and longing.

Ludwigshafen, January 10

Dear Ingrid,

The coming year shall mean only this for us: All stakes and strength for the work of the Kingdom. . . . Often my thoughts go to you in Africa and I long for you, but at the same time this longing spurs me on to double my work. The separation is easier for me, I know, because of my many duties, calls, and heavy schedule. You have much more time to think, to be quiet, to be lonesome. There are fewer distractions. Just that was the reason why I hesitated to tell you of my love. I didn't know which was the easier and which was the harder for you.

Yes, I still believe that "everything that is separated shall meet again." The only guarantee I can give you is the Watchword for today: "The things which are impossible with men are possible with God" (Luke 18:27).

Poli, March 6

These have been happy months at Poli, studying Fulani, teaching classes in French to the Africans, taking care of the sick, even going on evangelistic trips to the surrounding villages with my co-workers, Harriet Stovner, Reubin Johnson, and his wife, Millie. But now the Johnsons have to go to the States for a well-earned furlough. The Mission Conference does not want Harriet and me to stay on alone here at Poli after they leave. It's four hundred miles to our next station and we would have no means of transportation in case we needed help. We'll go to Meiganga where Ruth Christiansen, our expert in Fulani, will teach us more of that fascinating language. Also, I'll be working in the orphanage there with Ruth and Laura—doing the same kind of work Mother is doing in Bolivia.

Meiganga, March 30

The last child is in bed and now I "have the road" (as they would say in Fulani) to write you. This orphanage where we care for thirty-five children who have no mothers has been a living proof to the Africans of our message of Christian love. Most of these youngsters would have died were it not for the missionaries.

We take care of the little ones native style, to the best of our ability. The children eat while sitting in a circle on the floor around a dish of stiff mush which they pick up with their fingers and then dip into another bowl containing gravy. The babies remind me of little birds as they automatically open their mouths for food. Continually, I see that the missionary's job is much more than standing under a tree and preaching as I once thought it was; it's rather plain everyday living and loving.

I have been asked to teach the school for missionary children here at Meiganga. This will begin in September. I will have thirteen pupils in six different grades, including first year high school. This means I will have more than thirty classes a day to teach and prepare for. It is going to be a tremendous task, but I am happy about it. These children have a real future, and I am proud to be able to help them.

We also talked a lot about the Rey Bouba territory at our missionary conference. Personally, I can't help but feel a strong inner call to go there when the door is open. What do you think? Can we honestly face this challenge and ask God to make His way clear? Can we begin work there together?

Meiganga, June 8

You were wise to talk to Pastor Fuchs and I think he had a fresh approach to the problem. Remember? When facing a decision, instead of asking "Why do it?" he suggested asking yourself "Why not do it?"

Yes, do take the first step and write to the mission board. If God would have it differently, He will make it clear to us.

Garoua-Boulai, August 31

I can greet you now from my new headquarters. I'm living with Magda Pedersen from Denmark in one of the mud houses. It is the rainy season, and cold. One of the rooms in our house has been converted into the schoolroom. It will be a real pioneer school. The teacher's desk is made from a packing crate and the pupils' desks from native lumber. Only the books and supplies come from America.

I've just finished working out the daily schedule and my head is swimming. Thirty classes for which to make lesson plans and that includes high school courses in math, science, history, French, and English for my two ninth-graders. School begins at 8:00 and ends at 5:00, and there's still the preparation for tomorrow, so you can see how much time I'll have left to write to my prince.

Garoua-Boulai, October 1

Here's a good story for you to tell your friends about life in Africa. Last week Mr. Okland went on a buffalo hunt. For our Sunday dinner Mrs. Larsen made a delicious stew of buffalo meat and noodles. She left the kitchen for a minute. When she came back, she noticed something green floating on top of the savory dish. To her horror she saw it was a large lizard which had dropped into the boiling pot from the grass ceiling above. The lizard might have been poisonous so we were unable to touch the dish! So Florence had eight hungry people on her hands and nothing to feed them. We ended up with bread and guavas for our Sunday dinner!

Garoua-Boulai, October 14

Today is our engagement day. This much we know, that God has called us to work together. My heart is happy and yet, oh, so heavy, as I think of the thousands of miles between us and the uncertainty of the future. And then to have to pretend that this is a day just like any other, not to be able to share it with anyone here at the station.

Tonight I walked up and down the row of orange trees. Their heady scent hung in the air. The moonlight made the station a fairyland—and you weren't here! Please, let's get engaged once more after we're married and celebrate it properly together?

When I came home, Magda looked at my tear-stained face and asked me what was the matter. Even though you and I had agreed to keep our engagement a secret for a while yet, I couldn't hold back any longer. I just blurted out to her: "It's my engagement day."

Dear Magda, she understood so well. She smiled and said to me: "Well, if we were in Denmark we would certainly have a big celebration on such an occasion. But since we're not, how about the two of us having a small one together?"

So there we sat, under our thatched roof, sipping lemonade in honor of the day. She promised she wouldn't tell anyone else on the station. Then I read her a letter from Mother: "It makes me very happy to know about October 14. I pray that God may bless your lives. Also, that He will bring you together soon so that united you might serve Him in proclaiming the 'Good News' to His other sheep."

Garoua-Boulai, January 10, 1952

Thanks for your beautiful letter. You really took my breath away with your suggestion that I come to Germany for the wedding. But why not?

I can understand what this would mean to your parents, especially since they lost their only daughter during the war. And so through our wedding, you would like to give them back a daughter.

As far as "red tape" is concerned, marriage in Germany would certainly be the simplest.

Yes, marriage is a great risk—it's a plunge into the deep. But the greater the risk we take on God, the deeper and farther we dare to go from the safe shore, the richer shall be the treasures we will find and the greater the delights.

And I, too, know myself in oneness with you just as two bells opposite each other whose tones reach out into the distance.

Garoua-Boulai, February 17

Now I can tell you the date of our wedding: June 2, 1952, the date of your mother's birthday and of your parents' thirtieth wedding anniversary. Our Mission Conference has agreed unanimously that I be granted a temporary leave of absence upon completion of the school year. That will begin on May 9. Two days later I will be aboard a plane from Ngaoundere, have a short stop in Paris, and then on to the greatest adventure of my life: becoming the wife of Walter Trobisch!

Nine.

A German Wedding Ring

Things were happening fast. Now that our wedding date was set, everything else began to fall into place. At my remote African outpost letters came in from Germany, South America, and the States.

The first was Mother's, written from Arica, Chile. Her four-year term in Bolivia had ended and she was on her way to Santiago to board a ship for home.

Her last year at La Paz had been a lonely one. For the first time she was by herself, away from all her children. Mary had gone home to begin high school in the States. Then, a year later, twelve-year-old David had gone, too.

Mother had missed a lot of family events during those four years, such as John and Louise's wedding in 1948, Eunie and Vince's in 1950. In June, 1949, Paul graduated from Temple University. It had been a hard struggle to support his wife and two children, but with Ann's help he made it.

In that same month, June, 1949, John graduated from medical school at Washington University in St. Louis; I received my diploma in Paris; Veda finished her nurse's training at Immanuel Deaconess Hospital in Omaha; Carl graduated from Luther

Academy, and Gus from the eighth grade. All these events filled me with wonder. Even if our father had lived, and had been a rich man, he would have been hard put to it to pay all those bills for our education.

Veda had moved from Omaha to Rock Island after Gus's accident in July, 1949, where she worked as a nurse at Moline Lutheran Hospital. Renting an apartment, she made a home there for her younger brother and sister. At the same time she began working for her B.S. degree at Augustana College.

In the beginning the household consisted of Veda, Gus, and Mary. Then Marty came to begin her nurse's training at Moline Lutheran and Carl arrived to attend Augustana College. The landlady began to wonder when the family would stop growing. During this period Carl was invited to join a fraternity. He replied: "No thanks, I have my own fraternity at home." Just as the landlady thought that Veda had reached the saturation point, David came from Bolivia to begin junior high.

Now Mother wrote that she hoped to get to Rock Island in time for Christmas. Then there would be a day of rejoicing for the whole family—if not for the landlady. (But fortunately the landlady turned out to have a heart as big as her house, and she found room for all.)

Shortly after the holidays Mother received an invitation from John and Louise to visit them in Germany during the spring. John was there on his army service. They offered to help with the expenses of the trip. Mother would be able to attend our wedding in Mannheim. It was almost too good to be true.

But May 15 was still some distance away and I wasn't in the best of condition. A siege of infectious hepatitis the summer before left me weak and listless. The hot, dry season was just beginning. There were days when I could hardly lift my hand, let alone keep up with my grueling schedule.

But when our strength is not, God's strength just begins. Each day I looked at the Word over my desk: "As thy day, so shall thy strength be." Then, drawing a deep breath, I could go on.

After finishing my long day in the classroom, I stole away to the spring down in the valley. There I could just be quiet, seated by a little falls where the water ran fresh and cool. Overhead a giant acacia tree trailing its long vines formed an arbor which shut out the rest of the world. The song of the birds and the gurgle of the water over the rocks below soothed me.

In the evening, as I sat turning the little hand crank of my portable sewing machine, came my hour of pure joy. I had a wedding dress to make, as well as all the essentials for a complete summer wardrobe. With every stitch, the substance of dreams and prayers for the future became more real.

A few weeks later I sat restlessly in the train taking me from Paris to Kaiserslautern where Walter was waiting for me. To meet again after almost two years of separation! I tried to quiet my pounding heart, but it was no use. Then, as the train drew into the station, I saw him through the window. All was a blur—motorcycle suit, open arms, red roses. As I stepped out of the train it was a moment beyond description: now to meet in earnest the one with whom I would share my life.

Walter and I arrived at Pastor Fuchs's home late that evening after a ride on the familiar Trobisch motorcycle—a ride that stirred memories. On the door was a large hand-lettered sign: "HERZLICH WILLKOMMEN" painted across a map of Africa. I must have looked as though I had ridden straight from the Dark Continent. The cold cream I had put on my face as protection against the wind and sun served as an excellent dust collector while we sped through villages and along country roads.

We rang the doorbell. Who was the first to throw her arms about me but Mother! This was our first meeting in five years. And then followed the warm embrace of brother John. I had come just in time, for in a few days he and Louise would have to return to the States from Germany, his term as an army doctor at an end. None of my other brothers and sisters could be here for this reunion. But there were "Mutti" and "Vati," Walter's mother and father, who had just arrived from the Russian Zone. These were indeed the sweet fruits of waiting—to be once more united, coming as we did from the far places of the globe.

Then the busy time that followed. A few days later Walter wrote in our journal: "Here I am once more at the 'Standesamt,' the German office for the civil marriage required by law. This has taken a lot of time, and a lot of paper, and has cost a lot of money. Every official paper Ingrid sent me from Africa had to have two translations, because she was in French territory and the papers were in English.

"And the questions they've asked me here:

" 'Where was your fiancée born?'—'In Tanganyika.'

" 'Which part of Germany is that?'—'It's in Africa.'

" 'Is she a native?'—'No, she's an American.'

" 'Of what descent?'—'Swedish.'

" 'Where is her mother?'—'In Bolivia, South America.'

" 'What's *her* name?'—'Gertrude L. Hult.'

" 'What does the L. stand for?'—'I don't know.'

" 'Then you can't get your marriage license until you find out. In Germany no initial letters are permitted.' "

June 2 was the day of full surrender—each for the other—both for Christ!

We began the day's celebration with a festive dinner for our family and out-of-town guests. Those two hours were rich and memorable. There were toasts in honor of the occasion, table songs (Mutti wrote a classic in German, French, and English, relating the whole story of the Hult-Trobisch romance), and music by the Fuchs family. Most moving of all was the toast given by Walter's father. (It had been more difficult for Mutti and Vati to get a pass from the authorities of East Germany to attend their son's wedding, than for me to come from another continent.) For the benefit of the new relatives from across the sea, Vati reviewed briefly his son's turbulent life to date.

We were thankful to be able to have our wedding in the beautiful and reverent atmosphere of the Christuskirche, the only large Protestant church in Mannheim not damaged by bombs.

In the European tradition, we formed a wedding procession outside the church. Our little flower girl, Frohmut (the name means "happy courage"), was in the lead; then came the bridal couple walking side by side with the clergyman, followed by relatives and close friends. To the swelling strains of the organ, we moved slowly into the church and down the long aisle.

Walter and I were shown to our seats directly in front of the altar. But our chairs, instead of being together, were almost the width of the aisle apart, giving us a strange feeling of isolation. There we sat primly, shoulders erect, hands folded, pretending to listen to the wedding music. Then followed the moving sermon by Pastor Fuchs based on Isaiah 12: "Therefore with joy shall ye draw water out of the wells of salvation."

In the double-ring ceremony, according to custom, Pastor Fuchs placed our rings on our right hands. In Germany, as in the Scandinavian countries, it is the practice to put on the gold wedding band at the time of the engagement, but to wear it on the left hand; at the wedding, the rings are then transferred to the right hand. We had decided to abide by this custom—at least until we had received the good wishes of the guests. By that time our right hands with their newly acquired rings were paining us from the heartiness of the handshakes. Later we agreed we would wear our rings on the left hand.

Then came the honeymoon. (As I write this years later, it still hasn't ended.) Travel by motorcycle was cheap. We packed our sketchy wardrobe into an old canvas fold-up army bag and belted it securely on the baggage carrier behind my seat. Then with a thermos of hot coffee and our lunch in the saddlebags, we set out. For many carefree days we wandered over some of the loveliest country in Europe—through the Black Forest, beautiful Alsace, over into Switzerland from Geneva to Zurich, even spending five days in Arosa. And we did all this on a shoestring.

Happy though this time was, it was bringing us no nearer to

Africa. There were still serious questions to be answered before our purpose of serving as missionaries could be realized. At home in America we had a new mission board. Would they be willing to accept Walter sight unseen? And even if they did, would he, as a German, ever be granted a visa to enter French territory in Africa—especially in Cameroun where no German had been allowed to live since the first World War?

Neither of us had a salaried job, Walter having resigned as youth pastor. What would we live on until our commission came through?

We were confident, however, that some solution would be found.

While we waited, we accepted invitations to speak at churches in southern Germany.

Walter foresaw that he would need more training in French if his ministry in Africa was to be effective. In October we knew that our next step would be Paris. We had enough money to pay the railway fare to France and our rent for one month. That would leave us almost nothing for food. But in a spirit of adventure we decided to go ahead anyway.

We were having our minor problems in adjustment. During a youth retreat in Baden Walter had been asked by a pastor to take charge of the Sunday morning service in the village church. The sermon text was from Galatians 6: "Bear ye one another's burdens. . ." and one of his points was the importance of sharing.

Walter was working on this sermon one morning when I called him to breakfast. He was so deep in thought that I was unable to draw him into conversation. If I asked a question I got no response, or at best a mumbled word.

Finally, he reached over and took an apple from the fruit dish. It was a very special apple that a dear friend had given us, almost twice the size of a normal apple, juicy, red, the only one from a young tree. He cut it carefully in quarters. I asked for a taste of it. No answer. I watched the apple disappear piece by piece.

I couldn't keep back the tears. Walter realized something was wrong. I let him know that I was hurt because he hadn't shared the beautiful apple. He looked in astonishment at his plate where only the seeds and stem were left. He apologized. He had been so busy thinking about his sermon on "sharing" that he ate the whole apple without knowing it.

A week later we were in Paris. We managed to squeak by. But along toward the middle of November, the day came when I had to cash our last ten-dollar Traveler's Check.

Walter and I looked at each other. I went through my handbag and came up with a few francs for groceries. Walter dug into his pockets. All he had left were two subway tickets which would get him to his French classes and back. Now what?

The next morning I had returned from doing my marketing when the concierge stopped me in the hall.

"Deux lettres pour vous, Madame," she said.

I looked quickly at the envelopes. One of them bore the return address of the mission office in Minneapolis. Yes, this was it—the letter we had been waiting for. The other one bore the postmark of a small town in Germany.

Walter opened the one from America. Here was his letter of call from the mission board—and a check to cover our expenses while we finished our studies. The day was saved.

The other, too, was a letter of call, but to a church institution and retreat center in Germany. It was a generous offer, one which would mean a fruitful ministry for us both if we accepted. Now we had to make a choice. We needed God's guidance.

Instead of discussing the matter between us, we decided to read together the Daily Text as was our habit. Then in the light of God's Word each of us would take his notebook and in quietness and prayer write down the pros and cons of both calls. In this way we would seek to find the direction which God was indicating. Only after we had done this would we share our thoughts with each other.

An hour later we were ready. I gasped as Walter read what he had written down. With one or two minor exceptions, his pros and cons matched mine. Everything pointed in the direction of Africa.

Soon there was Christmas to look forward to. This would be our first one together. For weeks Walter had been telling me about his Christmases as a child and I always begged to hear more.

At last the December morning came when we could leave our tiny student room in Paris. A few hours later we crossed the French-German border.

That evening as we walked through a village, a light snow crunching under our feet, we knew we were in the land of Christmas. Every window held its candle. In a central place in each home and usually suspended from the ceiling, was an Advent wreath made of entwined evergreen branches and decorated with red ribbon and four candles. This was new to me. I asked Walter what it meant.

He answered:

"Advent, the preparation for Christmas, of waiting for the coming Lord, has been observed since the earliest Christians; traditionally, it has been a time of fasting, not of feasting. God wants us to wait for Him. To those who wait He will come. The symbol of waiting and coming is the Advent wreath. Therefore, Christmas really begins with the first Sunday in Advent, that is, around the first of December."

Then he described this Sunday and the Sundays that followed as his family had celebrated them:

"The room was darkened as we all gathered together in our living room. Ceremoniously, my father lit the first candle on the Advent wreath. Then we sang together the beautiful Advent and Christmas hymns, Mutti at the piano, Vati with his violin. Later we children too played instruments.

"The light grew from Sunday to Sunday as two, three, and then four candles were lit. The Light was coming closer. Darkness retreated. Then came the glorious moment when the full light of the Christmas tree flooded the room with its radiance, symbolizing the angel who announced the Good News to the shepherds.

"How well I remember that air of excitement filling the foggy December days of the Advent season! I always had a special Christmas calendar. It was usually a house with many windows—one window marked for each day of the Advent season. Every morning I could open one window and discover there the symbol or verse for that day. All of them pointed to the one day of fulfillment—the 24th, when the Christ Child Himself was to be seen. What a joy when I had the privilege of opening this window!"

We wanted so much to spend Christmas with Walter's parents. But they were in Leipzig, behind the Iron Curtain. We therefore accepted gratefully the invitation of Pastor and Mrs. Fuchs to join them and their children on Christmas Eve.

We felt the full holiday magic when we were ushered into their music room. In the middle of it the Christmas tree stood ceiling-high, all natural, all plain, the flames of white candles glowing softly above the green branches. This was the first time that members of the family were allowed to see the tree. It would remain in its place until Epiphany, the 6th of January.

Beneath the tree was a large stable, built by Eckart, the Fuchs's oldest son. Gathered about the manger were all the figures of the Christmas story lovingly modeled in clay, then baked and painted by Mrs. Fuchs and her children.

Eckart read the Christmas prophecies contained in the Old Testament and their fulfillment in the New Testament. We sang together the traditional songs as we sat in the semicircle around the lighted tree. Then we adjourned to the dining room where a simple supper—bread, butter, and honey, with cocoa to drink—was already laid out on the round family table. Instead of the hustle and bustle to prepare a fancy meal, we enjoyed an atmosphere of quiet peace and harmony as this family celebrated "Holy Eve" in their usual manner.

The second part of the evening was marked by a concert given by the family orchestra. All the children were gifted musicians, along with their mother.

No presents had been placed under the tree so as not to distract attention from the truly great gift of Christmas—the Christ Child Himself.

After that pleasant holiday interlude we returned to Paris, ready to buckle down to our studies once more. Walter enrolled for courses at the School of Theology at the Sorbonne, while I took some of the mission courses offered at the headquarters of the Paris Missionary Society.

In February we learned at last from the Mission Conference where we would be stationed. It was a remote outpost called Tchollire in northern Cameroun where no missionaries had ever before been resident.

The Lamido, or king, who had absolute dominion over his fifty thousand subjects, had, after many years, at last given his permission to establish the first mission station in Rey Bouba.

Rey Bouba! What magic doors of memory the very sound of that name opened for me! Father's copy of the Koran received during his visit with Baba Rey, the old king . . . Of course! The Lamido would be his son.

The prospect was exciting. We would be allowed to live where my father had traveled and where he wanted so much to return. Now perhaps his blighted hopes would be fulfilled in us. How strange—and yet how right!

We left Paris early one glorious morning in May. How our journey would end we didn't know. But to make sure that at least it began auspiciously, we circled the Arc de Triomphe on our motorcycle, not once, but three times.

When we stopped to fill the tank, the gas station attendant

asked us where we were headed. His eyes fairly popped when Walter answered nonchalantly: "To Africa."

The sea voyage was a pleasant one. It was the first anniversary of our wedding when finally we dropped anchor at Douala and got our seventeen pieces of baggage, including the motorcycle, through customs in record time.

We were in Africa together . . .

We interrupted the first lap of our thousand-mile trip inland to visit Cameroun Christian College at Libamba. Here we found young Africans with top scholastic records being educated through high school and junior college level. We visited one of the German classes and were amazed at what we saw and heard. An African student was translating a sentence nine lines long from Goethe's *Werther's Leiden* into perfect French.

The teachers were missionaries from France, England, Switzerland, Italy, as well as the United States. They worked together with a team of African professors in instructing the three hundred young students from thirty-six different tribes.

At Yaounde we reached the end of the railroad. From that point on, our way lay through the bush. Since we faced a journey of eight hundred miles and would be on our own, we decided to rent a truck with a driver.

Walter and I took our places in the cab with the African driver and we were off. Since I had been over this road before on my first trip alone upcountry, I enjoyed pointing out the landmarks.

The sturdy-looking truck proved remarkably fragile. We had to stop every fifteen or twenty miles because of motor trouble. At the end of the first day we hadn't gone very far. How long, we wondered, would it take us to cover eight hundred miles at this rate?

By driving fifteen hours the next day, we were able to limp into Garoua-Boulai, about halfway to Tchollire, during the evening. We were given a royal welcome by friends of ours—the Reubin Johnsons, the Cliff Michelsens (the same Cliff Michelsen whom I had known in Minneapolis), and the John Watnes, another missionary couple. Oh, what it can mean to see a friend's face in a far-off part of the world!

We didn't waste a moment in accepting Reubin's kind offer the following morning to take us the last four hundred miles to Tchollire in his own truck. We would send ours back. Reubin's truck, however, was smaller. Our baggage now included both the wood-burning stove and kerosene refrigerator I had used during my first term and which we needed at Tchollire. There was thus no room for the motorcycle.

The only solution was for Walter .to ride the Horex himself. I would follow with Reubin in his truck.

Our journey turned into a triumphal procession. Whenever the road led through a village, old and young would come running as the motorcycle appeared on the scene. They saluted stiffly, standing at attention. Walter returned the greeting by raising his finger to his sun helmet. No doubt about it: They mistook him for the advance guard of the governor. Then when Reubin and I followed a few minutes later in the overloaded truck, we would find the whole village still standing at attention! It was enough to make a queen envious! And as far as the baggage on the back of the truck was concerned, they would be most impressed. "What great riches they possess!" they would say to one another as they saw the old stove and crated refrigerator.

We planned to spend the weekend at Meiganga, where Walter could get acquainted with the missionaries. From Meiganga we would still have to travel two days to Tchollire, inside Rey Bouba, which was a kind of self-contained territory within the boundaries of Cameroun.

We had hardly fallen asleep the first night in Meiganga when we heard the sound of a heavy truck pulling into the station. Walter and I went outside, where to our surprise we found Cliff and Lil Michelsen. They looked haggard and worn.

We could not understand it, for it hadn't been long since we bade them a happy farewell.

"What's wrong?" we asked.

At first they could not speak. Then Cliff said:

"It's our little Priscilla-girl. She died just a short while after you left. We've brought her to Meiganga to bury her."

This was our first experience with the omnipresence of death in Africa. How could it be possible? Scarcely more than a day before I had held her warm little self in my arms. With all the wisdom of her two years she had pointed up at the moon and said proudly in French, *"lune."* Now, after a few hours' illness, she was dead. There was no doctor on the field to determine the cause. The nurse could only guess that it was some form of encephalitis.

Through their tears the parents said with composure:

" 'The Lord gave, and the Lord hath taken away; blessed be the name of the Lord.' "

Reverently we gathered for the funeral the next morning. Under a giant baobab tree we laid her as a precious seed in the African soil.

With heavy hearts we resumed our journey, this time over a high range of mountains, then again through green valleys. A crowd of monkeys whisked across the road and looked curiously at our motorcycle.

Thirty miles from our goal we came to an impasse. Owing to heavy rains, the dry-season bridge across the Benoué River was completely washed out. This was as far as the truck could go. The only way to get across was by a dugout canoe at the bank. I was poled over first by two Africans. Then Walter decided to place the motorcycle upright in the canoe and chance it. He settled himself in the middle, seeking to balance it, and clung to both sides of the dugout. The polers skillfully maneuvered the boat to the sandy shore, where I stood watching breathlessly.

And now came the last thirty miles. Without the Horex we never would have reached our destination. We often tipped over as we ran into sand. Once it threw us altogether as the back wheel sank over the hub in soft mud. But when we got it up again, it always seemed ready to go on.

At last we saw Tchollire in the moonlight. It was only a scattering of thatch-roofed huts upon an empty plain. Then somewhat nearer to us I could see four half-finished mud walls, projecting roofless against the night sky.

"What is that?" I asked.

"That skeleton," Walter observed, "is the house where we are going to live."

Ten.

Pagan Drums and Angel Chorus

We discovered one thing very quickly: We were no heroes. Dismay overwhelmed us as we stood there in the moonlight, gaping at the roofless building that would eventually be our home. Where would we sleep tonight?

Word of our arrival must have swept through the village, for we were soon surrounded by bobbing, smiling faces, all chattering volubly but incomprehensibly. We could scarcely understand a word they were saying. They seemed to be speaking Fulani, but the little of that language learned while I was at Poli had almost deserted me, and Walter knew none. This experience only increased our feeling of strangeness.

Suddenly, we were conscious of a consuming thirst. We longed for a drink, but we had no idea how to ask for water.

Just then Pastor Lloyd Sand and his wife, a missionary couple who had come here about a week before to get things ready for us, appeared out of the darkness. They had not expected us until morning. When we explained that our canteens had been emptied during our journey, he produced a small pail of boiled water and offered it to us. It had a strange smoky taste, but we gulped it greedily. At least it slaked our thirst.

Lloyd told us we would be able to get our water in the future from a water hole about half a mile from the village. But we would have to be careful not only to boil it but to filter it first, because it was filled with a kind of coffee-colored silt. This information depressed us even further.

He then took us to the guest house of the French administrator in the village where he had made arrangements for us to spend the night. He and Mrs. Sand would be here a few more days to see that we were off to a proper start at our new station, then they would have to leave on furlough.

The guest house was a straw-roofed native hut, consisting of a single bare room furnished only with two hard, bare canvas cots.

Tired as we were, Walter and I lay there tossing and turning, unable to close our eyes. Out of the African night came the eerie sound of beating drums.

We talked over our situation. It did not take us long to reach the conclusion that we were not up to the ordeal which lay ahead. We were not prepared in any way. We were not well versed in the language; we were inexperienced in making a life for ourselves under these unfamiliar, primitive conditions. We were failing in spiritual strength. But we were here. What could we do?

Then I had the happy recollection that our baggage and our household goods, our stove and our refrigerator, were not yet unloaded. They would still be waiting in the truck on the far side of the Benoué River, thirty miles away. And Reubin Johnson would be waiting there beside the truck.

Quickly we made our decision. We would admit our defeat. We would face up to our shortcomings, face the unpleasant fact that we lacked the Christian fortitude to go on. We would return to the riverbank in the morning, then go back with Reubin in the truck to the mission station at Meiganga.

Once we had made up our minds, we felt relaxed. Along toward morning we fell into an uneasy sleep.

In daylight, Tchollire presented quite a different face. The name, in Fulani, means "place of the birds." We were reminded of this when we woke up to a full-throated symphony. Going out to explore, we found the village tucked away in a valley surrounded by soft green hills. Blue mountains loomed in the distance.

The crisp air in the early morning was fresh and invigorating. But these blandishments of nature left us untouched. We had set our course and we would follow it.

The French administrator offered to rent us his truck to bring our household goods up from the river. We gladly accepted. But we had no intention of returning. We would send the truck back to Tchollire, then go on with Reubin.

Walter and I, jogging along in the truck with our motorcycle in the back, upheld each other in our decision. At last we reached the river. There was the broad expanse of the Benoué, gleaming in the sun.

Reubin sighted us as we approached and waved to us from the far bank. Then, as we took in the scene, we were filled with consternation. The truck was empty. Some of our boxes were piled on the near bank. Reubin and a crew of Africans had unloaded the truck. Even now our refrigerator and stove were being precariously ferried across in the dugout. We would have to break the news to him that we were returning to Meiganga, and ask him to go through all this work again in reverse. This prospect was almost as bleak as what we had faced at Tchollire.

We saw Reubin's white sun helmet as the dugout crossed the river, this time with another load of boxes.

He scrambled ashore in silence. He must have read our decision in our solemn expressions.

Then the three of us sat down under a tree while we poured out our hearts to Reubin. I will always be grateful for the wisdom of his counseling. He listened to us with sympathy and understanding, like a kind older brother.

When we had finished, he began to talk. He reminded us of all the years that the mission had prayed to gain an entry into this part of Cameroun, of the high privilege and responsibility that was to be ours as the first resident missionaries. He also reminded us of the thousands who were counting on us to succeed. Could we let them down because of a few physical hardships?

After a while Reubin and Walter went off to Tchollire in the truck. Reubin wanted to size up the situation for himself.

I remained under the tree awaiting their return. My conscience pricked me. I thought of my hardy forebears and their pioneering hardships on the snow-swept Nebraska prairies. Was I made of less sturdy stuff? I thought of Father and his undiminished courage. Could I break faith with his memory?

At last I heard the sound of the truck coming down the road. Walter and Reubin were both smiling. I knew then that we were all of one mind.

The next few days were such a busy time that we had no chance to feel sorry for ourselves. Reubin helped us store our household goods, then departed. The Lloyd Sands, too, would be leaving any day.

Our most exciting project was finishing our home, which would consist of two rooms with kitchen and one-room guest house attached. The two outbuildings were roofed over with grass and served as our temporary quarters. Our most urgent job was to complete the building of the walls and see to it that they were roofed over.

The building was being done by a man named Haldu, a mud mason and a genuine artist. Tall and stately, he came to work wearing a long white gown and red fez which he took off and placed under a nearby tree while he worked bare-waisted at fashioning the foot-thick walls.

Every day they grew about six inches higher. But each layer had to dry before another could be added. Alas, whenever there was a heavy rain, we could hear a disconcerting *plump-plump* as Haldu's unfinished walls came tumbling down.

Wai, the grass weaver, was also a master of his trade. He appeared daily, wearing a loose hip-length homespun shirt dyed in his own indigo vats. A fine-woven floppy straw hat almost a yard in diameter protected him from the sun.

Wai's first concern was to find the particular type of grass best suited for each job. A tall swamp grass, for example, was used for weaving the ceiling mat, which went on first over the bamboo poles tied securely in an inverted cone shape on top of the finished mud walls. Then he sent his men out to gather a strong field grass for the roof covering. They carried home great bundles on their heads. From a distance they looked like walking straw stacks. Still another kind of grass was used as cord to weave the long layers together.

At last Wai's work was almost finished. Layer upon layer of the woven grass had been placed in neat rows encircling the conical roof. And now came the nose cone—a huge mat woven loosely on the bias and resembling a Chinese hat—which was carried in a large roll up onto the roof and then fitted snugly over the layers of grass. Walter and I could only gasp in amazement as we saw the end product of Wai's expert craftmanship. We were told that a good roof made in this way would last ten years. Even the Lamido's royal palace was similarly roofed.

With the departure of the Sands, we were completely on our own. Each day brought new adventures as well as lessons in patience. One morning we had a caller, an old man in a ragged gown. He was waiting for me as I came out of the house after breakfast. We exchanged greetings. That went fine. All I had to do was reply *"Jam"* ("Well") to his endless inquiries:

"Are you well?"—*"Jam."*

"Have you slept well?"—*"Jam."*

"Is your husband well?"—*"Jam."*

"Is your house well?"—*"Jam."*

"Is your garden well?"—*"Jam."*

"Jam" was always the expected answer. Anything else would be an offense to Allah. If you ask a dying man how he is, he'll still answer *"Jam."*

There was something this man wanted. He repeated it over and over again, but since I could not understand him, I put him off as gently as I could.

"*Muyo sedda*" ("A little patience"), I said. "Wait a few weeks until I have learned Fulani better."

I went about my morning's work. I had not noticed that he went to sit down under a tree in the front yard.

At five o'clock I was surprised to see him still there. I sent our kitchen boy, Toma, out to ask what he was waiting for. Toma came back.

"The man said you told him to wait, '*Muyo sedda*.' That's just what he is doing. But he's getting tired now and would like to go home."

I never did find out what he had come for.

The mission station was built half a mile away from the village of Tchollire on a rise known as "elephant hill." We soon learned why it had that name. About a dozen of the great beasts paid us regular visits at night. We could not see them in the dark. We didn't have to. The ground shook as they thundered by. Sometimes they paused within a hundred yards of the house to pull up small trees with their powerful trunks and placidly munch the roots. The Africans assured us the elephants would never molest our house, and this was true. We did profit from their visits in one way, though. Our gardener didn't have far to go to look for fertilizer for our tomatoes, corn, and beans.

Life became easier when the building was almost done, for both the strong thick walls and the snug grass roof provided insulation against the tropical sun. We moved in while there were still only holes for the windows and doors. Walter and I struggled a long time before we got the window frames nailed together and covered with plastic screen. For doors we used the plywood sides of the refrigerator crate. We learned quickly that one never says "can't" on a pioneer mission station. There was nothing to do but go right ahead and tackle every job. Walter, who had always found it was easier to prepare a sermon than to pound a nail straight into the wall, was becoming a jack-of-all-trades.

It was an exciting moment when Haldu announced that he was about to "cement" the walls—the finishing touch. We watched every step with fascination. First he brought the bark of a certain tree, tore it into strips, and soaked it in water for twenty-four hours. This produced a slimy, gluey substance. Then he found little hills containing the excrement of the earthworm. He mixed these two, then with gentle motions of his hands smoothed it lovingly on the walls. We were amazed to see that it dried hard as cement and gave the walls a satin finish as well as protection from the rain.

One morning the workmen did not appear. They usually arrived just after sunrise, but this morning no one showed up. It was almost eight o'clock when Wai came running. He looked agitated and distraught.

"*Mbaroga don! Mbaroga don!*" he said excitedly.

We didn't know what the word meant. *Mbara,* the verb, meant "to kill." So we reasoned that *mbaroga* must be the noun form: "The one who kills." This in itself was enough to alarm us.

And, sure enough, Wai was crying: "A killer is! A killer is!" He babbled on in Fulani that he had just seen the bodies of a man and a woman. They had been killed by the *mbaroga* and their bodies half-devoured. He was trying to explain that this was why none of the men could come to work: the commandant had ordered them to organize a hunt for the *mbaroga*.

But what was the *mbaroga*?

On the assumption that it might be a wild animal, we took from the bookshelf a dictionary which had a section of illustrations. We showed it to Wai and asked him to point out the *mbaroga*. Without any hesitation he put his finger on the lion. At last we understood: A man-killing lion was on the loose.

Walter jumped on his motorcycle and went right over to the commandant's office. There he heard the whole story: This couple, it seemed, had been sleeping in their garden hut, which they often did at this time of year to scare the elephants away from their ripening millet. They must have heard a suspicious sound, their neighbors reasoned, and stepped outside to beat on their tin cans to scare off the elephants. But this time the marauder was no elephant, but a lion which sprang to the attack.

The tragedy had occurred only a few hundred yards from the mission station. Since the killer was still at large, it made us uneasy, to say the least.

All day the hunters were out beating the bush. But they could find no trace of the lion. Tension filled the air. The *mbaroga* could be expected to attack somewhere again tonight. Seventeen neighbors huddled together in our little storehouse. We tried to urge them to have faith in God, but it was clear that they preferred to put their trust in Walter's twelve-gauge shotgun. Walter and I hardly found it reassuring protection against a lion. After all, our bedroom had five large window openings. We could put our trust only in the God of Daniel.

About midnight we were wakened by screams. They seemed to be coming from the village. The lion must have struck again. We did not sleep after that.

In the morning we learned the grim story. Without warning, the *mbaroga* had crashed through the flimsy door of a native hut and quickly killed four members of a family. A little girl of eight cowered in the corner. But when she saw the *mbaroga* about to spring upon her helpless grandmother, she picked up a corn knife lying nearby and went after the marauder. The *mbaroga* turned and fled.

Word reached the capital. The Lamido sent his best hunters to join those of the commandant. All women and children were told to spend the night within the high walls of the Lamido's residence which he used only on his state visits to Tchollire. Once more the patrol went out. Still all efforts to find the *mbaroga* were futile. But at least on the third night there were no more victims as the professional hunters patrolled the outskirts of the village with their guns, spears, and bows and arrows.

As the next day wore on, we were all obsessed with one thought: What would happen tonight? Walter and I were uneasy as we sat down to our evening meal. We even noticed that as Toma came in, he was wearing what he called his *coupe-coupe*, his machete, fastened to his belt. He was afraid to walk the ten steps from kitchen to house without its protection.

I put off going to bed. I knew I could not sleep. Finally, before blowing out the lamp, I looked once more at the colored print above my writing table. It was the picture of an angel with outstretched wings guarding a small child. Underneath was the inscription in Swedish from Psalm 91:11: "He will give his angels charge over thee, to keep thee in all thy ways." With this reassuring reminder, somehow God quieted my fears. I fell asleep.

Somewhere around midnight I was suddenly brought wide awake. Not far off could be heard the cries of women and children. At the first sound my blood ran cold. Then, as I listened, I realized that this time the cries were different. Unmistakably, the villagers were yodeling with joy. This strange cheering in the night continued for at least half an hour. The meaning was clear enough. The *mbaroga* was dead! Now we could sleep in peace.

The next morning we were visited by a group that wanted us to come and see the dead *mbaroga*. Near one of the huts we came upon the body. The *mbaroga* was a female. She had been killed by a tall hunter of the Lamido as she was entering the village "seeking whom she might devour." The hunter pointed out a scar, indicating that she had been wounded by a bullet a long time ago. That may have caused her ferocity toward man. Also, once she had tasted human blood, there was no stopping her.

We had been on station at Tchollire for a six-week period that was far from uneventful. We had finished the house, continued to learn more of the language, and started a church. But even though we were official residents of his territory, we had not laid eyes on the Lamido who lived only thirty miles away in his palace at Rey Bouba. We were eager to meet this mysterious monarch.

The opportunity came when we received an invitation from the commandant to the celebration to be held on the 14th of July, the French national holiday. At the end of his invitation he had noted: *"Le Lamido sera présent."* That meant that the Lamido was coming to Tchollire. At last we could hope to have an audience with him.

How would the Lamido react to our being here? True, he had given his permission. But was he really aware of the implications? His father and grandfather had had the reputation of being the cruelest of all rulers in Cameroun. Would we find him any different?

The celebration of the French national holiday was brought off in great style. Most spectacular was the performance of the Lamido's warriors and horsemen. Such splendor, such colors, we had never expected to see in this isolated spot. First came a troupe of lancers wearing coats of mail and plumed helmets like the knights of the Middle Ages. Even their horses were decked in bright coverings of rich brocades. With the commandant, we were seated in a place of honor at the Lamido's right hand. The riders came galloping by in ever new arrangements, always reining up in front of the place where we were sitting.

Next came the archers, their brown skins blending in with their robes of deep, rich red. Cast over their shoulders were leopard skins with long, dangling tails. They danced for us, stomping and gyrating in rhythm. The drummers and trumpeters were clothed in white. All around stood the crowd. The varied costumes of the men were accented by the bright yellow dresses of the women. Beyond, shining in the morning sun, was the chain of mountains that shut us off from the rest of the world. Here was a little world all its own—original, true to nature, an expression of a unique culture.

Ringing loud above the spectacle, as though the colors could speak, was the music. Four huge, barrel-like drums, each strapped to a man's head and thumped by a taller man standing behind him, beat out the basic rhythm. Horns, with a plaintive two-tone melody, chimed in only to be drowned out by a tinny fanfare. Gourds of various sizes, resembling xylophones, added their melody. All the while the chief dancer, playing his mandolin, whirled around ever faster and wilder. Praises and shouts from the crowd, including the ear-splitting, long-drawn-out cries of the Lamido's wives, saluted him.

Then the warriors took positions for a ritual dance. They divided into six rows, three on each side. Alternately, they advanced and retreated as in mock battle. The front row consisted of the spearmen who crouched behind their shields and rhythmically went through the motions of throwing their weapons at the unseen enemy. Behind them was a row of noisemakers. With a wild array of rattling gourds, castanets, and horns, they made a hullabaloo evidently intended to keep the courage of the men at fighting pitch. At a generous distance behind them were the archers, quivers on their backs, and holding their bows in one hand. As they leaped in rhythm, the leopard skins covering their shoulders jumped with them.

At a sign from the Lamido, the shouts stopped instantly. Then, when the giant monarch stood up, the noise began again like the roar of the sea. To his subjects, this unapproachable veiled man embodied almost unlimited power. We saw now how easily this almighty father-figure could become identified in their eyes with their Supreme Being. For the first time we fully realized what it meant to announce our message here.

The next day we went for our first audience with the Lamido. We looked forward to the experience with mixed feelings. We were ushered through a dark passageway, then brought blinking into an open court. The Lamido stood before us, dressed all in white. Yards of spotless white muslin swathed his face and head, Arab fashion. We exchanged greetings in Fulani.

"*Jabbama!*" he said. ("Welcome!")

"*Min jabbi,*" we replied. ("We accept.")

His manner was cordial as he motioned us to a seat. He clapped his hands and summoned his interpreter-secretary. The man bent low as he approached and took his place, almost groveling at his monarch's feet. (The Lamido's subjects, we learned later, were forbidden to look directly into their ruler's face.)

The conversation began.

"Did you arrive well from your country?" the Lamido asked us in Fulani. His interpreter, Omaru, repeated the question to us in French.

Before interpreting our answer and almost under his breath, Omaru said:

"*Allah barkadini ma, Baba.*" ("May Allah bless you, Great Father.") Then he continued: "Monsieur says he arrived well from his country."

"Are you able to tell what is wrong when you see a sick man?" the Lamido asked Walter abruptly.

Again Omaru's preface to Walter's answer:

"*Allah barkadini ma, Baba.* Monsieur says sometimes he can tell what is wrong with a sick man. Sometimes he cannot."

The Lamido looked at me as he threw out his next question:

"Why are your children so much stronger than our children? I have heard they do not die so quickly." (We learned later the Lamido had a personal reason for asking this. In spite of his numerous wives, he had only three sons. And the oldest of these sons, in late adolescence, had recently died after a short illness.)

"*Allah barkadini ma, Baba,*" Omaru replied, "but Madame says perhaps it is because they are careful in feeding their children. The milk is boiled and here even the water is boiled to prevent disease."

"What kind of food do you give your babies?" he asked.

And so the conversation continued. From his questions it became clear to both of us that our "invasion" of his kingdom must be along practical lines, and above all, through public health techniques and medical aid.

Before the ceremonial exchange of gifts took place, we had the chance to tell our story. I described in detail my father's visit with his father. This story greatly impressed the Lamido. He said:

"You people have the Word of God and therefore also the strength of God. Continue to study it."

The Lamido must have heard the sound of the motorcycle as we had approached, for he asked us about it now. Walter went out and got the machine, then drove it in through the narrow passageway and rode around in a circle in the courtyard. The Lamido laughed like a child at the *tu-tu-tu*, as the vehicle is called in Fulani. But he wanted to know how both of us could ride on it. I promptly mounted the saddle seat and we rode around a few more times, to his great delight.

Among our gifts to him was a Swiss music box, which we had bought in Switzerland on our honeymoon for just such an occasion. When he opened the cover and it began to play, he clapped his hands in delight.

Among his gifts to us were some colorful woven mats.

We left with a sense of exhilaration. The first contact had been made. We were happy that his response had been a friendly one, for the whole of our success for our venture for Christ here in Rey Bouba would depend upon whether the Lamido was our friend or our foe.

One day Haldu lingered at the doorway. Finally, he got up courage to ask me to give him some medicine for his wife. I inquired what was wrong with her. From his description I concluded that she had a leg ulcer.

"But why doesn't she come here if she needs help?" I asked.

"She's afraid," he replied.

This made me feel bad.

"Would she be afraid if I went home with you and bandaged her leg there?"

"I don't know."

I thought I would try it anyway. Carrying my bag of medicines, I followed Haldu across the fields. He led us to his garden hut rather than to his main house. He and his wife had to remain there to protect their gardens from monkeys and elephants.

Two women were sitting apathetically in the smoky interior. Both of them were obviously Haldu's wives. He called to one to come out into the light. Her right leg was covered with a banana leaf. She explained that she had put this on to keep the flies away. After some urging she removed it, revealing an ugly tropical ulcer.

I cleaned it with a disinfectant, sprinkled some antiseptic powder on the sore, and bandaged her leg. I visited her twice in the next few days. Each time I won a little more of the woman's confidence.

The third time I went to change her bandage, I invited her to come and see me at the mission. Two days later I heard a knock at my kitchen door. Toma spoke kindly to her and came to call me. She smiled timidly and showed me her leg; the ulcer was healed. I invited her into the house. I showed her where we ate, where we slept. She followed me around shyly, saying nothing.

What interested her most was a little brown Teddy bear which Mutti had given me for Christmas. She jumped when I showed her how the Teddy could talk.

"Yonki don na?" was her question. ("Is there life in it?")

I assured her that there wasn't, that it was only a plaything. But I could see she wasn't convinced. A couple of days later she came back with her sister. She wanted to show her our "baby." She had even brought some peanuts as a gift for it.

That was the beginning of our break-through in reaching the women of Tchollire. Bandages and a Teddy bear had helped to overcome their fear of us.

Early one morning a man ran up, begging us to go at once to the little group of huts a few hundred yards from the mission. As we hurriedly followed after him, he told us that his wife had just had a baby girl.

"But the baby doesn't cry," the father said anxiously. "Can you help us?"

Walter and I looked at each other in desperation. What could you do for a baby who did not cry? Back in our bookcase was the obstetrics handbook that I had studied years before when I audited the nursing course in that subject. But there was no time to consult it now. Probably, I reasoned, as we went down the path to the huts, the baby was born dead, as so many syphilitic babies are.

Women were standing about in front of one of the huts. There was the baby, apparently lifeless, in the arms of an old crone. Another was dashing it with cold water from a gourd. The new mother cried pitifully as she looked at her baby. I took one look too and said to Walter:

"That baby's just one big mess."

The child, her umbilical cord dangling, was covered with vernix. Her body was cold. She must be dead. What could we do now? Without much hope, I examined the baby more closely. I caught a feeble heartbeat!

The minute I realized the baby was not dead, but only cold and strangling with mucous, Walter and I went into action. We wrapped her in a cloth offered by one of the women and ran with her to our house. With an ear syringe we began to clear the mucous from the baby's nose and throat. Then I started artificial respiration. At first it looked hopeless. But in a few minutes we were rewarded by a cry—a soft, kittenlike cry.

Quickly, I tied the umbilical cord. Then we wrapped the little girl in a warm blanket. We fixed up a box with another blanket and a hot-water bottle and put her in it. After I had wiped her face, I discovered underneath the vernix a really beautiful baby.

Half an hour later we took the little one, by now crying lustily, back to the hut. The mother was stolidly sweeping out, cleaning up after the birth. She stopped and looked at us, her face one beseeching question. Then, when she saw her baby alive and moving, she let out a heartfelt cry and embraced us in her gratitude.

That did it. Word spread from hut to hut that Monsieur and Madame at the mission could make dead babies live. Our medical reputation was now solidly established—alas, all too solidly, as the coming weeks would reveal.

One morning a pair of twelve-year-old boys, Sambo and Dumba, came to see us. They had walked over forty miles, they said, because they heard in their village that a mission was being started here. To our astonishment they informed us that they wanted to go to school and learn about the "Way of God."

Walter and I soon had a dozen boys at the station. He taught the beginners to read and write according to Frank Laubach's method of instruction. Walter's blackboard was the smooth mud wall of our house. I worked with the advanced pupils.

We had portions of Scripture available in Fulani. What a change I noticed as the boys discovered they could read these by themselves. Fullness instead of emptiness, a goal instead of aimless living, truth instead of superstition . . .

Every Sunday twenty-five to thirty people from the village gathered in our little round-hut chapel. They sat on small logs. The day Walter preached his first sermon in Fulani, using the text, "Jesus said, Follow me," the sermon was thirty-six words long. With much repetition he was able to stretch it out over all of two minutes. The next Sunday, however, we were astonished to see that the attendance had doubled. This tantalized us. We could not be sure whether it was in spite of, or because of, the short sermon. One thing, however, was certain: The people wanted to hear.

To announce the Gospel exacts a high price. We were reminded of this anew when a telegram reached us from Cliff and Lil Michelsen. It carried the sad news that their little son Mark had died at the age of eight months. Only nine weeks after they had laid their little Priscilla in the African earth, they laid Mark beside her. What did God mean by it? We did not know, unless it was to show us the earnestness of the task to which we were called.

By now our mornings were almost entirely taken up in caring for the sick. Before we even finished breakfast, there they were, thirty or forty of them from all the villages around. We did what we could with our rudimentary medical knowledge.

Our missionary doctor, stationed one hundred and fifty miles away at Ngaoundere, sent us medicines by mail along with detailed instructions. He encouraged us by saying: "Ninety per cent of the people you can't help, I can't either."

First we sorted out our patients: those who came for worm medicine, those with tropical ulcers, those with venereal diseases (a high percentage, another of the "blessings" the white man has brought to Africa), those with sore eyes (what wonders a tube of antibiotic eye ointment could perform!), and those in need of dental care.

Then as we wrote down the names of our patients and the kind of treatment given, Toma played our portable phonograph with Fulani records sent to us by Gospel Recordings. We found these records to be very effective. As the speaker explained the story of creation, he interrupted himself frequently and said to the listener: *"A nani na?"* ("Are you listening?") Invariably the patients would answer in chorus: *"Oho, min nani."* ("Yes, indeed, we are listening.") In time we trained one of the boys to help us. We prayed for the day when a nurse would be stationed at Tchollire and a real dispensary built.

Walter and I found it important to have a neat and tastefully furnished home in which we could relax after these exhausting mornings. Our two rooms, with the beautiful picture on the wall, the fresh vase of flowers, and even the brightly decorated table, helped to restore us after the heart-rending sight of human suffering.

In the afternoon we each taught our classes; afterward we looked forward to the twilight hour.

Sometimes Walter went hunting to get some meat for our schoolboys; sometimes we went visiting in the village; but for the most part we were content to pull up our camp chairs in front of the house and wait together, glass of lemonade in hand, for the first star. It appeared just above the highest peak to the west.

Then came a creative pause. It was too dark to work, and still not dark enough to light the lamp. We used this time to think back over the day, talk abou. the mistakes we had made, what we should have done differently, and discuss our plans for the next day.

To keep our mental balance we purposely planned activities in the evening unrelated to our mission work. We had brought with us a few choice phonograph records. Our favorite was Mozart's *Kleine Nachtmusik*, and with this we began our quiet hour. Sometimes we played games together or made music on our little portable organ. Usually Walter read to me whenever I tried to catch up on my sewing: Sherlock Holmes in English, a recent French play, Dostoevski in German. It was very peaceful. Outside we could hear the singing of crickets in the still African night.

The great event of the week was the arrival of the mailbag. One day a letter from Veda brought us news of her commissioning service in August, 1953, at the Fridhem Church in Funk, Nebraska, where our great-grandparents had been charter members.

Clippings from our church papers described her call and commission:

"There were few dry eyes among those who listened when Veda Hult told the mission board why she wanted to go to Tanganyika as a missionary. Simply, but feelingly, the clear-eyed, sweet-faced nurse explained how she had been deeply moved while a young student at Luther Academy, when Mrs. George N. Anderson told of the spiritual needs of the people of Africa. A week later came tidings that Veda's father, who had returned alone to Tanganyika in the midst of World War II, had passed away at Dar es Salaam. 'I guess that decided it,' she said simply. 'I wanted to carry on where he left off.' "

Her commissioning was a special day in our family history, too. All five brothers were brought together by the occasion for the first time in ten years. Mother, home on furlough from South America, was there too. In fact, Eunie and I were the only members of the family unable to be present. (She was in Pakistan studying Pushtu with her husband Vince.)

Several weeks later another letter from Veda brought word that she had landed at Dar es Salaam. This was ten years after our father's death. She was the first member of our family to visit his grave. Veda wrote of her experience:

"Pastor and Mrs. Schoedt, a young couple from Denmark, brought me out to the cemetery today where Daddy is buried. As we gathered around the grave, Pastor Schoedt led in prayer—one of thankfulness and praise to God. That evening as the sun was setting I had a walk along the Dar es Salaam harbor. The words from Hebrews 11:4 came to mind: '. . . he died, but through his faith he is still speaking.' "

Her letter made Veda seem so close to us, yet we were actually almost three thousand miles apart.

While Veda was busy with her first adjustments to life at Wembere station in Tanganyika, Walter and I were making plans for our first Christmas in Africa. This year it would be our unique privilege to announce the Christmas message in an area which up till now had never heard it. How would we go about it?

Even our own observance presented problems. I wanted an Advent wreath, but there were no evergreens. I found a length of old hose and bound it in a circle. Then I covered the hose with some gauze bandage we had received in a missionary package. By pushing four large darning needles into the hose I was able to anchor the red candles, one for each Sunday in Advent. I placed it in the center of our living room on a small table. On Walter's birthday, November 29, we lit the first candle and sat in silence as we watched it flicker and then burn steadily. To us it was a symbol of the first light glimmering at Tchollire.

Since the dry season was here, and the rivers had now receded, we could plan a trip by motorcycle in mid-December to Rey Bouba to see the Lamido and share the Christmas story with him.

We sent word of our request through his representative. To our great joy he invited us to come.

We were met outside the walls by his horsemen, who were clothed in chain mail. Like knights of the Middle Ages we rode expectantly through the covered gatehouse into the almost medieval town.

With great formality we were ushered into the Lamido's throne room. We set up the flannelgraph and in Fulani began to tell the Christmas story, illustrating it with our colored pictures. The Lamido sat cross-legged on his throne (an elaborate brass bedstead covered with a rich Oriental rug) and listened attentively, full of expectation, as a youngster listens to a thrilling adventure story. Several times he interrupted to ask us about the Child in the manger. When we had finished he said:

"I would like you to tell this story to all the people of Rey."

We were astonished. The Lamido was a Moslem; his advisers were Moslems. Why was he willing to expose his subjects to Christian teaching? We could only speculate that perhaps somehow we had reached him.

Upon the Lamido's order, all the dignitaries of the town assembled in the open court in front of his palace. Solemn and venerable, and wearing long white robes, these men came to the meeting place and sat on the ground.

As we retold the Christmas story in this outdoor setting, we realized anew how thrilling it is. The long way to Bethlehem . . . the inquiry at the inn for shelter and the refusal . . . the shepherds in the field . . . and then—the Child in the manger.

For this fascinated audience it was as if we were reporting a recent event, and the pictures a literal recording of its truth.

The session ended with much handshaking and many friendly exchanges. We made ready to start for home. Outside, next to our parked motorcycle, what did we see but a beautiful Arabian horse! A servant of the Lamido was standing beside it. He stepped forward and in Fulani, relayed to us this message from the Lamido:

"Thirty years ago the father of Madame visited the father of the Lamido. Madame's father at that time received a horse. Today the Lamido wishes to repeat this action. The Lamido also wishes to give you a copy of his holy book, the Koran, in remembrance of this day."

Walter and I looked at each other in consternation. We were happy to have the Koran. But what on earth could we do with a horse? The Lamido, however, had done us a great honor and paid tribute to my father as well as to his. To refuse the horse would be an insult. We accepted it as graciously as possible. It would be delivered to us at the station.

We returned to Tchollire on our motorcycle. The Lamido sent a slave with the horse the next day. We gave the horse the name "Sedako," which means "witness" in Fulani. We kept him tethered to a tree not far from our house, and visitors flocked from the village to congratulate us on the Lamido's generous gift.

There was just one more day to get ready for our own Christmas. We unpacked the box of Christmas decorations and the small artificial tree we had brought with us. Toma helped us make a little native stable out of dry grass and pieces of woven mats. In it we placed the figures of the manger scene. Young and old came to admire it. Then our tree was set up and bedecked with glittering ornaments. The villagers' eyes grew wide.

The stars were out. The wind rustled in the leaves. Yet, at first, it didn't seem much like Christmas Eve. We longed for the Christmas songs, the snowy streets of Germany.

Then we reminded ourselves that our Christmas Eve here must be not unlike that first Holy Eve on Judean hills. We both felt better as we sat in front of our mud house and looked out at the beauty of the African night. That star over the highest mountain peak was gleaming as brightly as though it were the Star of Bethlehem.

In our hearts we heard the angel chorus bursting into song. But our ears heard only the beating of the village drums. To us these drums were a reminder of our call to be God's messengers in a land that had never before heard the angels' song.

Eleven.

Battlefronts

We had just packed away the Christmas decorations when the mail came. Among our letters was one with a Denver postmark. The news it contained left us numb. John's wife, Louise, the mother of three, was dead.

Only a few days before we had received a Christmas letter from her with word about their children. Margaret was four, Eleanor, two, and Danny, six months. She had written enthusiastically of their plans: "John finishes his residency at Denver General Hospital in June. He hasn't made up his mind where to locate, but is now investigating opportunities for pediatricians. We like the West, so we'll probably stay in this part of the country."

Now she was gone. The love and concern of brother Paul and his wife who were living in Denver at the time helped John through those difficult days.

Mother's furlough was ending. She was in Rock Island and packing her suitcases to return to Bolivia. But when Paul called her, she changed her plans at once and took the next plane for Denver. A week later, Mother wrote us from there:

"John was weeping, but quiet, when I arrived. He has a firm, abiding faith in God which is seeing him through. He knows there is much for him to live for, so he's brave, though his heart is very sad. He has so many friends who are sharing his sorrow. A woman working at the hospital told him she wants to come and baby-sit on her day off so that I can get out.

"God has made it clear where I'm to be now. John wants to keep his home together, so I've promised to stay as long as he needs me. And I do enjoy these lovely children. It's fun to be a homemaker without having to be a breadwinner too."

John wrote a tribute to Louise which was read at her memorial service at her home town in Illinois:

"No human pain has ever been as sharp and deep to me as the loss of my beloved Louise. Each morning now begins with an agonizing battle to escape the reality of her departure. 'No!' I pray. 'This can't be true.' Yet we all know it is true. God has seen fit to call her away at a time when we felt that we needed her most. . . ."

And then Veda's letter arrived from Tanganyika:

"It's a month now since the very sad news came of Louise's death. It is at such a time as this that one especially longs to be with the rest of the family—and to share or help in some way. It is so hard to understand 'why' but again we need not ask or understand the 'why,' knowing that our Heavenly Father doeth all things well.

"I'm so thankful for the six weeks I spent in Denver with Louise and John a year ago. I really enjoyed Louise and grew to love her dearly. She told me of her childhood, of her time in nurse's training, etc. Once she spoke of their days in Germany, of Walter's being with them and the blessing it had been to her and John. How my heart aches for John! May God who alone is able use even this that his faith might increase."

We could scarcely believe it when, several weeks later, we received another letter from Mother:

"I have wonderful news for you. John has applied to the board to go to Tanganyika as a medical missionary. A month after Louise's death, he broached the subject to me. I knew he was much in prayer and meditation, so in a way I really wasn't too surprised. He confided to me that he wanted to offer himself, but he didn't know what to do about the children. Under no circumstances could he leave them.

"I told him how only two days earlier the same thought had occurred to me: 'What if John should want to go to Tanganyika?' Then it had dawned on me that I could offer to go along and take care of the children. But I left it in the Lord's hands. I resolved not to mention it to John first. I never dreamed it would come to a head so soon."

A few days later there was a letter from John:

"God has done much in the past two months to ease the terrible pain which the untimely departure of my beloved Louise brought, both directly and through the warm love and sympathy of loved ones and friends. I needn't tell you that Mother's presence has afforded a wonderful pillar for me to lean on.

"The Heaven-sent directive which is turning our compass toward Africa came as clearly as if it were written in neon lights. Since then I've begun to experience an inner peace and joy which I've really never known before. In so many ways I feel inadequate for such a grave yet exciting responsibility of bringing physical and spiritual help to those who need it so badly. The attractive offers and opportunities for practice here now have absolutely no appeal for me."

At Tchollire the weeks passed quickly. Attendance at the Sunday morning services had doubled. There were now as many sitting outside of the chapel as there were inside. The villagers expressed their desire for a larger *Sudu Allah* (House of God) and began to collect materials for building one. On their own initiative they gathered stones, brought bundles of grass, roof beams, and bamboo poles.

One day in the heat of the noonday sun, Dingale, a soldier of the commandant, came running to our house.

"My brother Joseph," he panted. "He is dead."

Walter expressed our sympathy. Then he asked:

"How did it happen?"

"He left Tchollire this morning on the government truck for Garoua where he had a new job. The driver went around a curve too fast. Joseph was thrown out, the back wheels ran over him, and he was killed."

Joseph had become a Christian while attending the mission school in Garoua. Only last week he had announced that he wished to give up his work with the government to study medicine. This very morning he had sent us a farewell letter. Now he was dead.

His body was brought back to Tchollire for the funeral. Dingale asked us to take part in the burial service at five o'clock the same afternoon.

When we reached the burial site, the sun was already low. It would soon disappear behind the mountains. Then we heard an extraordinary sound, one that moved us deeply. The mourners, instead of wailing inconsolably, as was their custom, were singing hymns. When they had finished, Walter gave his message of consolation about life after death. He spoke in French, and his words were translated by two believers into Fulani, and into Sango, another tribal language.

Dingale stepped forward and asked if there were any present from whom his brother had borrowed money. If so, would they please forgive him the debt now at his graveside? Then the body, wrapped both in a white cloth and in a grass mat, was lowered into the ground. All came forward and threw handfuls of dirt into the open grave.

Sadly, we returned to the station. Joseph's untimely death was a tragedy. But it never occurred to us that it would also open the way further for the message of Christ to reach the people of Tchollire.

This Christian funeral, the first the local people had ever seen, made a deep impression. Instead of indulging in the death dance, and giving way to mourning and wailing, a group gathered in the village evening after evening to sing and pray. Others came and listened, for here was a great mystery: How could Africans face death so joyfully?

Dingale called on us again. This time his face was beaming. He himself was not yet baptized, but he had brought with him three men, all pagans, who wanted to confess Christ. Then he handed us a list of nine others. They asked us to hold a meeting in the market place to explain the Way of God. Others, too, were eager to accept this belief which took away the fear of death. Many came to our outdoor meeting the following Sunday afternoon.

In a few weeks our new *Sudu Allah* was finished. It had no walls; the sides stood open to the elements. But the roofing was superb. It had cost us all of fifteen dollars. More than two hundred attended the inauguration. Afterward, we had a picnic. Using our wash boiler and kettles, Toma and I cooked rice, which was served with peanut oil to everyone.

The heavens had continued a hard smooth blue, with never a cloud to break the heat of the sun. During the day the temperature rose to 120° Fahrenheit and never fell below 90° at night. The land lay before us, no longer green, but dead-brown, and thirsty.

We felt the need to get away for a while. We were delighted when Cliff and Lil Michelsen invited us to spend our vacation with them. Cliff came for us in his pickup truck.

It was good to be in the fresh, clear air of a higher altitude. How we enjoyed the cool nights! And how we enjoyed, too, the fellowship with our missionary family at Meiganga!

Two important decisions were reached while we were there attending the annual conference. The first: Two Africans, André Garba and Paul Darman, who would become the first pastors of the Sudan Mission, were to return with us to Tchollire. They would be of great assistance to us both in evangelization and in our school work. In return, Walter would teach them. Here would be the beginnings of a seminary which our mission hoped to establish later at Meiganga.

The second decision: A missionary couple whom we did not

know, Ernest and Helen Johnson, now studying in France, would join us at Tchollire within a year. Ernie would initiate the industrial school, and Helen, a trained nurse, would take over the dispensary.

Lil and I had many good talks. One Sunday afternoon we placed flowers on the graves of Mark and Priscilla under the baobab tree at the mission compound at Meiganga. We prayed once more that the sacrifice of these young lives might bear fruit for the Kingdom.

In our talks we shared our innermost desire, which was that each of us might have a child. Our conversations revealed that both Lil and I had been warned by our doctors that it was most unlikely. But, we asked each other, couldn't God work a miracle even here? We made a prayer pact that each would remember the other in this heart petition.

After a delightful month Walter and I returned to Tchollire. Everything appeared to have been running well during our absence. Outwardly we seemed to be making substantial progress. Then one day an incident occurred that made us wonder if we hadn't been deluding ourselves.

Paul Darman, who was helping with the afternoon classes, appeared suddenly one day, quite out of breath.

"What's the matter?" asked Walter in alarm.

"Everybody's left!" Paul gasped. "They've all gone from the station."

Walter was aghast.

"I can't believe it!"

"It's true—even Toma, your faithful helper."

Paul pointed toward the village.

"Look—you can still see them going along there with their mats and possessions."

A long single line of villagers with bundles on their heads was moving slowly down the road.

What on earth could have happened?

Just then, André Garba came running up.

"Quick, Monsieur!" he cried. "We must stop them and find out what is wrong."

Walter jumped on his motorcycle. André mounted the seat behind. They speedily overtook the moving line. Walter shouted at them to halt. Stolidly, the men and women continued as if they had heard nothing. Then André dismounted, snatched the bundle from the head of the first man, and with sheer display of force succeeded in bringing him and those behind him to a halt.

"What's the matter, Anea?" Walter asked.

"It's no use, Monsieur," Anea shrugged.

"What's no use?" Walter demanded.

"We cannot live any longer with you at the mission or try to follow the Way of God. See those mountains over there?" With a gesture, he indicated the blue range in the distance. "Our sins are like those mountains—equally as high, equally as great. That is why we have decided we all must leave. It's impossible to obey God's Commandments."

Only then did Walter grasp what had happened. First they had learned all the Ten Commandments by heart. Then at night around their fires, they had learned the meaning from Paul and André. Slowly, head knowledge became heart knowledge. Suddenly they realized that to put the Commandments into practice would involve a drastic change in their lives. When they concluded that this was impossible, they could see no alternative but to return to their heathen traditions. But if they did so, they would have to leave the station.

Finally, Walter and André persuaded the villagers to go back home. With troubled faces and shuffling gait, they turned on the trail and retraced their steps.

The incident filled Walter with dismay, until he realized that complacency had been disturbed, apathy broken. Now was our moment of opportunity.

Many good conversations followed as Walter counseled with them individually. He explained to them Jesus' words when He said: "They that are whole have no need of a physician, but they that are sick. . . . I have not come to call the righteous, but sinners to repentance" (Matt. 9:12; Luke 5:32). Now for the first time they could understand the Gospel of love. But first had to come this experience of the law.

We were encouraged by the progress to extend our frontiers. In June, Walter organized a trip to Sasa, a village to the southeast of us accessible only on foot. He described it in his journal as follows:

"Rain is pouring down as we reach Sasa on the afternoon of the second day. My horse whinnies when it sees the tops of the grass huts appearing on the horizon. In the fifty-mile distance from Tchollire we have passed no other village. We spent the night in the bush under the stars of the open heavens. Today the path has taken us over high mountains. Now we arrive—ten carriers, my horse Sedako and I—tired and wet.

"The chief has to be called from his garden. He is bashful and somewhat embarrassed because he is dressed only in a dirty loin-cloth. I try to behave as 'unwhite' as possible, in other words, to be friendly, to shake hands, to speak softly, to demand nothing, to hurry no one, to have patience. In short—to do everything that would not be expected from a white man.

"The chief ushers me into a round hut about seven feet in diameter, which is in his compound. Evidently it has served as a kitchen and is still smoky.

"In the evening I am called to a bigger hut to greet the elders. We agree to have a meeting the next morning, before everyone leaves to work in the gardens.

"The gong wakes me. When I come into the main hut it is already filled. Everybody sits on the floor, the women with their children tied on their backs. The chief presides over them, his throne a wobbly chair.

"We begin with a hymn. Most of the carriers have their noses deep in their song books to give the impression that they can read.

"The great moment has come. These people have never heard

.the Good News. This is a situation to be envied.

"I tell them first the story of the Prodigal Son. They listen intently. The enticement of a large city in a far country; leaving the home village in order to live better—all that they understand well. As I tell of how the son wastes his money in a few days, they respond with a knowing smile that speaks of experience. They can't get over the fact that in my flannelgraph pictures the pigs are eating out of a basin—an unheard-of luxury.

"And then the great call: 'God waits for you . . . you people of Sasa, as the father waits for his son. He will receive you too, in His Kingdom. God has not forgotten you. He knows you. He waits.'

"When I pause, the chief starts to speak. He challenges his villagers to follow God's road. Then he preaches a short sermon, probably more effective than mine.

"I ask Wajiri, one of the carriers, to pray. Immediately there is a disturbance. I had forgotten that these people have never prayed! Wajiri has to explain it first. Heads are bowed, eyes closed, hands folded. But it still does not become quiet. The women are giggling and explaining to each other how to do it. Finally they calm down and Wajiri leads them in the first prayer of their lives.

"The next meeting is held later in the day after their evening meal. It is not raining this time, so we gather on the street. I try to make Jesus great to them, describe how He was: His birth, His deeds, His death and resurrection. I realize that especially toward the end, when I talk about death and what comes afterward, I have aroused their interest. To them, this is the main question: Their lives are filled with fear of death. I decide to tell them tomorrow the story of the Rich Man and Lazarus.

"I have made no mistake. The next morning as they listen they follow the story silently, intently, almost solemnly. Their hearts are wide open to the message of eternal life. Heaven and hell are realities for them—not abstract concepts. The meeting ends with a call for decision to follow the way that leads to heaven.

"When we pray this time everyone is silent before God. The Word of Life has reached Sasa. The seed is sown in one more village."

On another occasion Walter and I went on a trip, together with our carriers. Our motorcycle would be useless, for it was the rainy season. The uncut grass towered over our heads on what were supposed to be roads. Besides, there were uncounted rivers to cross. But we brought our horse Sedako and took turns riding him whenever our feet would carry us no farther.

I thought of my father as I jogged along over the same trail he had ridden so many years before. He had been a pioneer, making a pathway in the wilderness. Now we, his children, could walk in it and reap the fruits of a long-overdue harvest.

Nor were Walter and I alone. To the north, to the west, and to the south of us, beyond the borders of Rey Bouba, five missions were at work; in my father's time there had not been a single witness.

Whenever we entered a new village, we would make it clear to the chief that we came not to take but to give. By late afternoon he would gather the people to hear us as they came from their gardens. At first they would be suspicious. Hadn't most white men come to get their peanuts, their cotton, or even their boys? What were we really after?

Walter would explain how we had journeyed from a far country, how we had traveled fourteen days and fourteen nights in a boat with a strong engine, and many days by train and truck. Great astonishment . . .

Then Walter would turn to Toma, Musa, Wajiri—who were in the first baptismal class and who hoped to be baptized at Christmastime. They could speak from experience about the power of the Commandments. Slowly, the suspicion would be dissipated.

Christmas this year took considerable preparation. We held the first baptism at Tchollire of five young men and one woman. The light that had begun to glimmer last Christmas now burned steady and strong!

We were busy, too, fixing up living quarters for Ernie and Helen Johnson, who would be arriving in March. But first would come the annual conference at Meiganga. There I would see Lil Michelsen again. I was so eager for her to know my good news. Walter and I at last would be blessed as parents.

My joy was therefore doubled when I heard Lil's news. The Michelsens, too, were expecting a child in May. And so our meeting together this time was not unlike that of the two cousins, Mary and Elizabeth, many centuries before. God had honored our prayer pact and we were thankful.

One morning Walter and I stood at the dusty airport in Ngaoundere, waiting anxiously for the first glimpse of the silver bird in the sky that would bring Ernie and Helen. At last, there it was.

Helen was the first to come down the gangway. She looked beautiful with her slim figure, long, loose blond hair, and blue eyes. Then we saw Ernie staggering under the load of winter coats and all the pieces of hand baggage which the practical-minded missionary insists on taking along. The coat pockets bulged with bolts and nuts, and from them protruded the handles of wrenches, pliers, and screwdrivers.

During their first weeks with us the Johnsons were entirely immersed in intensive language study. Then they joined their efforts to ours. Walter concentrated on literature and evangelization, while Helen and I managed the dispensary and the women's classes. Ernie worked on the building and teaching program.

With our forces doubled at Tchollire we could function with greater effectiveness.

At Tchollire we were now encircled by three hostile fronts. One front, to our sorrow, was the Lamido. Although he still appeared to be friendly, we began to sense that he regretted having granted missionaries permission to enter his country. Evidently he had not foreseen the explosive power of the Gospel. Not long after Walter had returned from his successful trip to Sasa, the Lamido summoned him and warned him sternly not to undertake such trips in the future without official permission.

Mysterious things began to happen.

One after another, our helpers were called away from the mission and ordered to work in another village. Our friend, the commandant, was replaced. There were many depressing incidents. But saddest of all was the experience involving Musa.

One day Walter was ordered to appear before the Lamido. After the ceremonial greetings, the Lamido asked him if he had a boy named Musa living with him at the station.

"Yes," Walter answered, "he takes care of the horse which you gave me last year."

Walter could not see the Lamido's expression, for only his eyes were visible.

"Did you know that Musa's father was a child [slave] of my father?" the Lamido asked.

"No, I didn't," Walter replied.

"That means that Musa is my child," the Lamido said. "I ask you to return him to me."

"What do you wish to do to him?" Walter asked boldly.

"I wish to teach him the ways of my kingdom," the Lamido answered.

Walter returned to the station. His heart was heavy as he called Musa to him—Musa, who sang happily as he fed the horse; who attended classes regularly; who remembered easily the Bible stories he had heard; who learned how to pray, in a childlike touching way; who fled from his village when his father died; who came to us, asking that we be his parents so he might be free.

When Musa heard the news that he must go to the Lamido, he burst into tears.

"It's a lie!" he sobbed. "They will not teach me! They will put me in jail and beat me because I lived with you."

It was heart-rending. We could see clearly now the spiritual battlefront: The forces of Islam coming down from the north, of Christianity up from the south, were locked in conflict over this child.

Musa sat on a grass mat, leaned his head against Walter's knee, and wept inconsolably.

We were at a loss to know what to do.

Slavery in northern Cameroun is forbidden by law—on paper. But in some areas, such as here, the French administrators tolerate it silently to keep peace with the native chiefs. To refuse to give back Musa would mean to destroy the good relationships we had so painstakingly developed. And it might even make the Lamido an enemy of the mission. If this happened, he could very well close all doors to future, as well as to present, work.

Walter summed up how he felt about it in our journal:

"I knew the battle would begin someday. But has the hour already come to start the fight? If so, are we ready for it? Has our work at Tchollire been deeply enough rooted?

"I decided we were not ready. I did not dare to set out the tender plant of this small church, risking it against the storm of persecution by the Moslems. For the sake of the other Christians I would have to sacrifice Musa.

"As he sat before me on a mat, weeping, I thought of Onesimus, the slave whom Paul sent back into slavery to his slaveholder, Philemon. But Philemon was a Christian. The Lamido was not. Was Musa well-enough equipped to withstand the pressures to which he would be subjected?

"I reminded Musa of the story of Joseph in the Old Testament, who also was sold into slavery and who went through troubles and jail until God's plan was revealed. This should comfort him —it did not excuse me. I felt like the betrayer who sold one of his own to Egypt for the sake of a cheap peace.

"I took Musa personally to the Lamido. He was clad only in a pair of shorts. His belongings, his money, he had left with us. 'They will just take everything away from me anyway,' he said.

"Musa had to wait outside. The Lamido did not receive us together. I tried to show the Lamido my interest in Musa and asked him not to do him any harm. I said that I wished to be kept informed about him. This the Lamido promised. I left. Musa entered the Lamido's compound. The door closed behind him.

"I said to myself, 'I have failed him. But God will not.'"

Our second front was the French administration. Just as Jesus was thrown back and forth between Pilate, representing the power of occupation, and Herod, the local authority, so we, too, often felt we were being thrown back and forth between the French commandant and the African Lamido. When Ernie first filed an application to open an industrial school at Tchollire, for example, he was referred from one to the other without receiving permission from either.

The third front was the threatening one of heathendom and of superstition.

Ndiya, wife of Yaya, Helen's cook, was pregnant. She had just started to read God's Word by herself, when she was ordered to return to her home village by relatives. Her tribe held the belief that if she, a pregnant woman, sprinkled the blood of a sacrificed chicken over the garden of her father, the peanut-stealing monkeys would be chased away. We refused to let her go on the hazardous journey.

At Tchollire a young couple were expecting their first child. When the mother went into labor, she was forced to sit upright on the dirt floor of her hut. If she lay down, it was believed the baby would get water up its nose and drown. For the same reason the poor girl was given nothing to eat or drink. Our objections were in vain. Her labor became prolonged, and the mother died of exhaustion before the birth.

We were all devastated by this needless loss of two lives.

One day we heard that twins had been born in the village. We knew that the parents would consider this a curse. We hurried to visit them and congratulated them on the two beautiful girls.

Africans often ask us missionaries to name their children, feeling that it confers prestige. We named the twins Maria and Martha. But the father was pessimistic.

"You know what this means," he said with a sigh. "Because of these twins, someone in the family will die. Better it be one of them."

We tried to convince him that the twins were a blessing of God. We visited them often, taking gifts. But we soon saw that Martha, the firstborn, was the favored one. It was she who was always first at her mother's breast. Her cheeks were round and full, while Maria grew steadily thinner, and was often ill. One day the mother described to us symptoms that sounded like pneumonia. We asked her to bring Maria to us for treatment. She did so.

I went to prepare a shot of penicillin. Then I called out to the mother to bring Maria in. I gave the injection without noticing the baby's face. Then I discovered it was not Maria at all, but Martha. I scolded the mother for her trickery, but she had no bad conscience. Martha came first in everything, even penicillin shots.

When Maria recovered, I asked the mother if she wouldn't leave her in my care at the station. But she shook her head sadly.

"Maria is not my child," she said. "She belongs to the chief. I am a slave. The chief gave me to the man from whom I have these children. They belong to him. Any day the chief can give me as wife to another man. . ."

And so it went with one incident after another.

The months of waiting for our baby passed quickly. In the midst of them came the joyful news that Cliff and Lil Michelsen had a son. The boy was the first missionary baby to be born in the newly completed hospital at Ngaoundere. And soon it would be my turn to go there for the birth of our baby.

I looked about me to find something that would serve as a baby basket. How about the *Reisekorb* (journey basket) that we had brought from Germany? Of woven reed and fitted with a cover, it had been useful as a trunk. I removed the cover, replaced it with mosquito netting, lined the inside with soft muslin, and made a mattress out of an old blanket. It was all ready for its occupant.

The baby was due in August, during the rainy season. We would have to travel one hundred and fifty miles over bad roads to get to the hospital, not to mention crossing the Benoué in a dugout at floodtide.

We planned the trip carefully. Ernie and Helen would take us as far as the river in their pickup truck. Dr. Eastwold would meet us on the other side and take us to the hospital at Ngaoundere. But so many things could happen. If it should rain hard on the day we left, the route would become impassable. If the doctor hadn't received our letter, there would be no one to meet us. And then, too, the baby might arrive sooner.

But when the time came to leave for the hospital, the day was clear. We were off before dawn, and reached the Benoué by seven o'clock. Dr. Eastwold was on the far bank in his carry-all. I was greatly relieved to see him.

Walter crossed first with a part of the baggage in the leaky dugout. The *Reisekorb* containing all the baby clothes was sitting in at least six inches of water. At last the dugout came back for me. It was a risky journey. The water seeped in at a faster rate than it could be bailed out. The polers, as they had done on the previous crossing, stuffed old rags in the cracks with a knife. I crouched in the bow and looked out over the river. It seemed immense, and the other side so far away.

I closed my eyes and prayed that all would go well. Then when I saw we were approaching shore, a great wave of happiness engulfed me.

The long trip to Ngaoundere was a breathless race with a rainstorm. We managed to keep just ahead of it. We were barely safe under the missionary doctor's roof when it struck with all its force.

I was drying out the *Reisekorb* and its contents when I felt the first labor pains. Now that we had reached our haven, the baby was losing no time.

Hand in hand, Walter and I experienced this hour of birth. It will always remain for both of us one of the greatest hours of our lives.

The gasoline lantern hissed. The two nurses moved swiftly in the spotless hospital room. The doctor spoke quiet words of confidence. With each mounting contraction I turned to look at the *Reisekorb*. In a few more minutes it would be empty no longer.

I fixed my mind on the special promise God had given us this morning from His word: "He who asketh, receiveth."

The moment came. The strong hands of the doctor lifted the little one into the light of the world.

"It's a girl," he announced.

And her lusty cry filled the room and our hearts.

Twelve.

Behind the Iron Curtain

"*Usoko, Usoko, Allah barkidini mo.*" ("Thank you, thank you. May God bless her.")

"*O nandi baba mako . . . bingel manga . . . gasa mako dudi . . . kine mako boddum masin.*" ("She looks like her father . . . such a large baby . . . with so much hair . . . and what a good nose.")

For us as parents, the words of Martin Luther, "Where you see a child, there you meet God in a new way," proved to be true.

Each day we marveled anew at the power of God's creation in our Kathryn Herta. We had named our daughter after Walter's sister. It seemed that others too were meeting God in this child. Every day African visitors, many of them from faraway villages, came to see her, bringing gifts of eggs, chickens, and peanuts. They always left with the heartfelt wish: "May God make her to grow up!" We found this touching, for it was not always realized in their own children.

One day five tall carriers appeared, each with a large basket on his head. They brought rice, peanut oil, wild honey, eggs, and woven mats. The Lamido had sent them with presents for the new baby. We were pleased at his thoughtfulness and always welcomed any contact with him that would aid in our work, even if it was only temporary.

He also sent a request that Kathryn be brought to his palace the next morning. So, dressed in her best, even to wearing shoes and socks (which never failed to draw comments from African onlookers), we took her on her first royal visit.

As an ambassador of good will, she behaved admirably. Kathryn won the Lamido's heart, and he did not hesitate to tell us what great joy she brought to him.

Through Kathryn, too, I soon found new avenues of approach to the mothers. Being one gave me an authority I'd never had before. Tragedies in childbirth, owing to ignorance, had to be overcome. Helen and I decided to begin classes in prenatal care.

Helen opened the sessions by showing the women charts of the baby in the womb. When they saw that the child was upside down, they exclaimed in surprise. Then Helen showed them how the baby lived in fluids before birth. Eventually, we were able to dispel their fixed idea that the child would drown should the mother take a reclining position during labor.

Even the relation of the menstrual cycle to conception was a revelation. They had been taught that a difficult period meant that a chicken was scratching inside the woman's stomach; also, that labor pains were caused by the child in trying to break cords which bound it to its mother so it could be free!

The day came all too soon when Helen and I had to put into practice what we were teaching. Ndiya was about to have her first child. She had been engaged to Yaya from babyhood, but only last year was she pronounced *"bendi"* ("ripe" for marriage). We guessed her age at fourteen or fifteen.

We had first suspected she was pregnant when she appeared at the dispensary one day and asked for *"lekki tutugu"* ("medicine for spitting"). When we inquired if she was "with a stomach," she shook her head. Not until after a visit to her home village did she admit it. Her mother-in-law, the village midwife, had pronounced her "with a stomach for one moon."

"When did she say you would have your baby, Ndiya?" Helen inquired.

"When the millet heads bend over and are ready to be cut."

That would mean about the middle of December. Just to make sure, when Dr. Eastwold came on his regular visit we asked him to examine her.

"About the middle of November," he said.

Helen and I looked at each other. Who was right?

It was a struggle to keep Ndiya from returning to her home village, as was traditional. We knew a curse would be on Yaya's head should she die in childbirth in any village but her own. He would be held responsible. As punishment, he would be locked up for three days in a hut with his wife's body.

This was our dilemma: Were we really being fair to Yaya in insisting that Ndiya remain with us?

In November we received another urgent call from Ndiya's village, insisting she be sent home. Her people did not consider that she would have to walk forty miles, and swim or wade at least a dozen rivers. Again we said no. Walter and Ernie both admitted they would be relieved when this baby was finally born.

Then Yaya's mother showed up. At least, said Ndiya, we ought to let her mother-in-law be present at the birth. We agreed on the compromise, not foreseeing the consequences.

Ndiya had been in labor for twelve hours before anyone told us. By that time Yaya's mother, as midwife, had tried all her skills.

She began by rubbing her own arms and legs with kerosene.

"Why did you do that?" I asked.

"Because the evil spirits fear that smell. It's a white man's smell."

Poor Ndiya! When Helen and I entered her hut, there she was, sitting on the dirt floor, her mother-in-law alternately massaging her abdomen with peanut oil and pounding her on her back.

"I'm trying to help the baby break its cords and come out quickly," she explained.

All our pleas that Ndiya be brought to the dispensary went unheeded. So we had to make the best of it in the dark, crowded hut.

We slid a clean mat under Ndiya, then sponged her off. We had a hard time persuading the midwife to wash her hands with soap and water. She agreed only because soap gave off another white man's smell which the evil spirits wouldn't like. Then we tied a white apron around the waist of the midwife, who was wearing only a loincloth and a few beads. Even Ndiya had to smile.

The contractions were coming only a minute apart. At any moment the child's head would emerge. But nothing further happened. Ndiya looked faint.

"I have no more strength," she whispered.

Helen and I became alarmed. I bent over Ndiya and spoke softly and rapidly to encourage her. The midwife had no patience with talk. Stepping forward, she thrust her fist into Ndiya's mouth. The poor girl gagged. Protesting, Helen and I pulled her away.

"Why do you do that?" Helen wanted to know.

"Dole on" ("It's force"), the midwife said with a shrug. If the mother gagged, then the baby would be forced to come out. Next, she used a gooey substance taken from the bark of a tree, which, she said, would prevent tearing when the baby was born. The atmosphere was tense. Were we working together, we wondered, or each against the other?

At last the baby's head appeared, and, a few seconds later, the rest of the body. It was a girl.

Then came the real excitement. Ndiya began to weep. The midwife told us it was because she didn't hear her baby cry. That, we knew, is the African mother's greatest fear.

Struggling to ward off the midwife, Helen managed to clear the mucous from the baby's nose and mouth. At last we heard a sound no louder than the mewing of a kitten. Helen quickly wrapped the baby in a cloth. She guessed her weight at little more than four pounds.

Next came the ceremony of cutting the umbilical cord. Yaya was called to participate, as was customary in his tribe, the Duru. Solemnly, he took out his knife, cut off a small section of the bamboo roof pole, carved it according to his mother's instructions, and handed it to her. She made a circle with it three times in the air, then she severed the cord. Helen tied it, sterilized it, and dressed the baby, while I took care of Ndiya.

It was all over. Walter and Ernie came in to admire the newborn. We named her Maria. They said they couldn't decide who looked more exhausted, the mother, or the three midwives—two amateur and one professional.

It was time for our first furlough. Ernie and Helen were now seasoned hands, so we had no worries. Also, Pastor and Mrs. Ellingboe would take our places when we left.

Our little Kathryn would soon be a year old. Walter's parents were waiting eagerly to get acquainted with their first grandchild. After visiting them, we would go on to the States. It had been almost eight years since I left my family and friends.

Thanks to the airplane, we made the transition from blistering Fort Lamy, on the edge of the Sahara, to cool, comfortable Frankfurt-am-Main in a day. Quiet weeks of rest in the Odenwald healed our battleworn nerves. We sat for hours on a quiet hillside, reveling in nature's autumn glory.

Mutti had obtained a pass from the Russian Zone. She and little Kathryn soon became fast friends. One morning we watched them leave together on the Inter-Zone train for Leipzig. We knew Kathryn would be in good hands in her grandparents' home while Walter went on a round of speaking engagements and I awaited the birth of our second child.

Two months later Daniel Martin (named after his two grand-fathers) gave his first cry to the music of Mozart's *Kleine Nacht-musik* in the delivery room of the Deaconess Hospital in Mannheim. A tape recording of his arrival was made for Walter.

When our son was about a month old, Walter and I had an opportunity to go to Leipzig to spend Christmas with Mutti and Vati. For the moment restrictions were slightly relaxed; we could get an Inter-Zone pass. But the Suez crisis was at its height and the revolution in Hungary was still raging. Ought we to take the chance?

Then Mutti wrote us that Vati's health would prevent their coming to West Germany for the holidays. I read the Watchword for the day: "He who observes the wind will not sow and he who regards the clouds will not reap." In my notebook I wrote down: "Go to Leipzig." When Walter came home the next day from his speaking tour, he showed me his notebook. In it was written: "Leipzig: *Ja*."

Our son Danny began his travels with the long train ride from Frankfurt. He timed his feeding just right. The train had stopped for border control (we had to cross the Iron Curtain—a section of no man's land with the guards and watch towers). As the tough customs officers and policemen entered our compartment to check our papers, they saw a nursing baby. It had a strange effect. Their voices grew hushed; they quickly backed out the door, wishing us *"Gute uceise."*

During the trip Walter pointed out the historic landmarks. The first was Wartburg Castle where Luther had translated the Scriptures into German. We passed through Eisenach where Luther had first attended school, and then through Erfurt where he had become a monk.

Dusk was falling as our train drew in. Vati was waiting on the platform. His eyes filled with tears of gladness as he bid us welcome. This was the first time, since that day ten years ago when he had escaped with only his knapsack, that Walter had been back in his home town.

Walter showed me the scenes of his boyhood, such as the school he had attended, while we rode in an ancient taxi to his parents' apartment. Where buildings had been destroyed by bombing only an open space remained. The rubble had been carted away. Or what had been rebuilt was only a façade to give an impression of prosperity.

Leipzig, long famous for its annual trade fair, was also a book and education center. Because of visitors from West Germany, the shop windows looked enticing. But I was told that inside, counters and shelves were almost bare.

We stopped in front of the gray four-story apartment building on Windscheidstrasse, where bullet marks still remained from street fighting during the war. On the second floor we rang the doorbell, and there stood Mutti with our little girl in her arms. Now it was my turn to weep. For three months we had been separated. How often I had ached to hold Kathryn in my arms once more—and at last I could do so!

Kathryn pointed excitedly at her baby brother. She was the picture of health with her rosy cheeks, shining eyes, and golden hair. It was a happy homecoming. My first impression of Leipzig had been one of grayness. But here within the shelter of these walls, where so much of Walter's childhood and youth had been spent, all was light and harmony. We were glad then that we had neither "observed the wind, nor regarded the clouds."

That was the beginning of five amazing weeks—amazing to me, first of all, because of the spirit of the people we met, friends of Walter and his parents, a spirit both irrepressible and contagious. I never heard them complain, although they had reason to do so. The opposition of the State only made their faith all the stronger.

How else could one account for the fact that seven thousand people gathered every Sunday in Advent in one of the largest churches in Leipzig to hear the Christmas message, although the service could not be announced publicly?

I went one day with Mutti to a Bach concert at the famous

Thomaskirche where the composer played and where he lies buried.

The huge audience that came to hear his *Weihnachtsoratorium* sat motionless before the majesty and power of Bach's announcement of the Messiah.

I could better understand afterward why one pastor called Bach "the fifth evangelist," ranking his ministry with that of Matthew, Mark, Luke, and John because of the way Bach had interpreted, through his music, God's message to mankind.

Many essential foods, including milk and butter, were strictly rationed. Mutti would sometimes have to wait an hour for her daily allowance of one pint of milk, which she gave to Kathryn. I was not allowed any because I had an American passport. We had brought powdered milk from West Germany, so Danny and I got along fine on that.

A pastor's wife told us of the great excitement the day a shipment of oranges arrived at their neighborhood store. After waiting in line she was able to buy two apiece for each member of her family. But, she said, it was worth it. The sight of those oranges caused real jubilation.

In the evenings some members of Walter's former youth circle in his church slipped over to visit him. Secretly, by word-of-mouth, it was arranged one evening that they all meet together at the home of one of them. Walter and I related our experiences in Africa. Then they revealed some of their problems to us. Each wore the insignia of the Christian youth group: a cross against a circle denoting the world. To be seen wearing it, we learned, was to invite trouble. Their courage made us humble.

Among those present were a woman doctor, a pastor, a music teacher, a printer, and several public school teachers. Each in turn described what it meant to live a life of faith in conflict. The children suffered particularly. In the morning they were taught in the State school that Jesus never lived, that all stories about Him were fairy tales. Then, if they had Christian parents and attended the pastor's classes later in the day, the children heard the opposite. This spiritual tug of war was demoralizing.

A few days later we were invited to the home of Dr. Ihmels, the director of the Leipzig Missionary Society, one of the oldest and largest in Europe. My father had corresponded often with Dr. Ihmels during his work in Tanganyika after the first World War. On his way back to the States in 1926 Father had spent several days in Leipzig, reporting on his work in the field. Dr. Ihmels remembered Father well and we had a good visit together.

The Christmas festivities were over all too soon; it was time to return to West Germany. We were sorry to have our good times with Mutti and Vati come to an end. But we had much to look forward to. In a few days we would sail for home on the S. S. *America.*

It was snowing on the cold January day when we prepared to leave. We bundled up our two babies. As Walter carried the suitcases down to the waiting taxis on Windscheidstrasse, I lingered behind for a few moments. I took a long look around at these rooms where we had spent such happy weeks together—the rooms where Walter had grown to young manhood. Reverently, I closed the doors behind me. Some instinct, some intuition, told me that they were now forever locked. I would never enter them again except through fond memories.

With our children on our laps, Walter and I rode through the sad, gray streets of Leipzig. We could see Mutti and Vati in the taxi ahead. How kind, unselfish, and considerate Vati was. I thought of the many sacrifices he had made, often standing for hours in a queue to buy us choice tickets for a concert, an opera, or a play.

One of these was a first-run play, *Abraham Lincoln,* written by a Leipzig history teacher. It was a fair presentation of the martyred president's life story, but it carried the implication that the American nation had been unfaithful to his ideals.

Vati was smiling at Mutti. I knew so well that special look he had for her. It always warmed my heart to think that after thirty-five years of marriage a man could still gaze so adoringly at his wife. But who could help loving little Mutti with her quick mind and contagious humor, always ready for new adventures?

She was concerned about Vati. He often had a pain in his heart, and at night he would walk the floor to relieve it. But he never said a word to us and kept up the pretense that all was well.

Again I thought: "Lock this scene forever in your memory. You will see it no more."

Thirteen.

Reunion

We woke up to a rumble of cranes and a grinding of winches. During the night the S.S. *America* had pulled into the landing docks at Southampton. Walter and I were filled with expectancy. Eunie and her family were on their way home after a long term in Pakistan and we had arranged to meet them here.

We watched the tourist-class passengers as they came aboard. I saw no one I recognized. In a few minutes the gangplank would be drawn up.

But wait! I thought I caught a glimpse of two little girls trudging slowly up the gangplank. One of them had bright red hair. Could that be Ann, Eunie and Vince's oldest? And the one with her—Edith, the blond four-year-old? Just then I saw Eunie, leading two-year-old Ruth by the hand.

I ran to meet her. In a twinkling we were in each other's arms. The stewards looked on in amazement. You had reunions when you got off a ship, not as you boarded one! And next came Vince, grinning broadly under his Persian lamb cap and carrying their new baby. They told me that little Alice had joined the family on January 1.

We could have stopped right there on the deck of the S.S. *America* and sung "Praise God from Whom All Blessings Flow." But there wasn't time. A steward took the family away to their stateroom. Walter turned to me and said:

"Ingrid, she's beautiful—your sister. And so calm and composed. Why, you'd think she was on her way to a concert instead of just having made a trip halfway around the world with a two-week-old baby, not to mention three other children."

Perhaps it was the aura of new motherhood that made Eunie so radiant now. But I felt, rather, that it was because she knew the secret of the Shepherd who will "gently lead those that are with young" (Isa. 40:11). The strength that she and Vince had been given for such an undertaking was beyond their own.

Her composure was all the more remarkable because their trip had been a harrowing one. Eunie told me of it later as she nursed the baby in a lower bunk.

They were traveling against a deadline. Vince planned to enroll at Augustana Seminary on February 1. This meant they had to leave their station, the mission hospital in Pakistan, by January 15 at the latest.

As with most home-bound missionaries, their last night had been spent packing. When all their gear was in the hospital station wagon, they bade tearful good-bys to their co-workers and friends who stood shivering in the chill of the early morning.

"*Puh mush day shuh!*" ("May God go before you!"), those staying behind called out.

"*Amin to sera! Khoday day Khpul berkut werkuh!*" ("The same be to you and may God give you His own peace!")

The children waved as the station wagon turned north to Peshawar where they would make connections to the coast. Eunie and Vince were especially saddened to leave behind them their saintly co-workers at Tank, three English women whom they had learned to love. They knew they might never meet them again.

One of these, Dr. Maidie Sherbourn, was a veteran of forty-three years of missionary service. Twenty-five years ago she had begun this hospital with Ethel Haddow. Later they were joined by Vera Studd, niece of the famous British missionary, C. T. Studd. Vince and Eunie were assigned here after finishing their Pushtu language study. Vince worked as an evangelist among the male patients and villagers, and Eunie helped with women's work.

I asked Eunie what the country was like and what kind of people lived there. She replied:

"It's a unique and remote region of the Northwest Frontier Province whose rugged hills and mountains form the border between West Pakistan and Afghanistan. The people are called Pathans. They're proud and independent, and very tough. They have to be—life is hard in their territory. The rocky hills are dry. They're blistering hot in summer and bitter cold in winter."

"How can the people possibly make a living in such a place?"

"That's just the trouble. When a man can't get enough from his field to feed his family, that's all the excuse he needs to loot and steal from his more fortunate neighbors on the plains below or from the caravans crossing these borders.

"Blood feuds between families or whole villages result from this desperate struggle for a living. The people believe one death or injury must be avenged by another."

Patients at the Tank mission hospital often came in with gunshot wounds, Eunie said. A man might be shot while he was working in his field, tending his flock, or otherwise going about his business. The patient, if he was able to speak, often asked the doctor to fix him in a hurry because he wanted to get even with his enemy.

And all these years Dr. Sherbourn and the other courageous missionary women had worked faithfully at that unrewarding post. With great skill and meager supplies they battled an unbelievable array of illnesses and injuries, always holding uppermost in their hearts the desire to proclaim the God who dwells, not only far off in heaven, but here among men, "near to all who call upon Him."

Eunie sighed as she laid the baby, now peacefully sleeping, in her carry-cot. I could see how desperately weary my sister was, now that she was beginning to relax, and my heart went out to her.

She continued the story of their trip. They had made a day's detour by car to say good-by to their good friends, Bishop and Mrs. Jens Christensen. After welcoming the family Mrs. Christensen took the three tired children to a room where they found three small beds, freshly made up, and a table their size all set for supper in front of the blazing fireplace. The girls really loved that.

Late into the night Eunie and Vince visited with the Christensens and talked of the young, struggling Pakistani church. The Christensens, with other workers of the Danish mission to the Pathan tribesmen, had labored here for thirty-five years. They studied the languages, learned to know the people, translated the Scriptures, preached, taught, and gave medical help, undaunted by the high cost to them in sickness, loneliness, and heartbreaking disappointments.

They made the supreme sacrifice the day they discovered their only son, John Martin, a lad of eight, knifed to death by an enraged Pakistani while the boy was playing in their own backyard. And yet they continued to serve without bitterness. The Christensens had a special place in their hearts for Eunie and Vince, for they were about the same age that John Martin would have been.

The last thing Eunie and Vince did before leaving the next morning was to pause at the small cemetery not far from the Mardan church, where they stood silently at John Martin's grave. Then it was back to Peshawar where they boarded the train.

They had to spend two nights and a day in a small railroad compartment as the train took the little family to Karachi. Their journey was further marred by an unexpected accident. The heavy shutter of the train window fell down suddenly on Ann's hand. One of her fingers was broken. Having nothing with which to disinfect it, Eunie wrapped it in one of the baby's sterile diaper pads.

The first thing they did at Karachi was to find a doctor to look after Ann's hand. (I noticed she was still wearing a splint on her finger.) He also treated Eunie, who was fighting a breast infection.

Then came the thirty-hour plane ride, touching down at Kuwait, Baghdad, Istanbul, Rome, and London. They had traveled with the sun, so for them it was the "longest day."

But these anxieties were forgotten now that we were together.

The five days and nights of the voyage would be far from long enough for the talking we had to do to catch up on our eight-year separation.

Walter and Vince never tired of swapping stories of their experiences among the Moslems.

"How was it with you, Vince?" Walter turned to his brother-in-law as they sat talking together one day in the tourist-class lounge.

"I was terrified when I saw my first tribesmen," he said. "They are tall and erect with strong features and piercing black eyes that ask: 'Who are you and what do you want here?'

"My job was to contact them in the bazaars. Each day I spent many hours there in the local teashops, and in garages and flour mills. We usually began by discussing the weather, or who had a new camel, or who had killed whom and why. Then we'd be brought our tea. As the last bitter drops were poured from the cracked old teapot, and we drank it together, we'd usually get to talking about the Christian faith. And then I would present to them the Gospel of love, so different from the hate and fear which were a part of their daily lives."

"Did they listen to you?"

"Oh, yes, they'd listen. But if any did make the break with Islam, it meant almost signing their own death warrant."

Vince paused.

"So your efforts seemed futile?" Walter asked?

Vince shook his head.

"You know, Walter, it gripes me when people at home measure our success as missionaries by counting the number of converts. If they hear there are only a few in a certain field—such as ours, for example—they think it would be better for us to go somewhere else, where we might achieve more visible results. But I am not of this opinion. When we have an open door to preach, the results are none of our business. Our job is to get the message across. God will give the increase."

I wished so much that my father could have heard this conversation between two of his sons-in-law.

We were busy getting our baggage through customs when we caught sight of Carl. It was good to see this tall brother of ours after so long. In the interim he had graduated from Luther Academy, then from Augustana College, and had completed his two years of army service in the Intelligence Corps.

He was working in a New York office, and studying voice during his spare time. Carl had always loved to sing, and was considering music as a career. But he wasn't sure yet—perhaps God had other plans.

Quiet but friendly Carl had a tenor voice that could melt a heart of stone—especially when he sang one of his father's favorite Swedish hymns: "Flee As a Bird to the Mountain." As a boy, he used to sing when he milked the cows down in the hollow at the Homestead. When Mother heard him through the open windows of the cottage, she would go about her work smiling.

Carl was laughing when he met us.

"This morning," he said, "I asked my boss if I could have the day off so I could come down and meet the *S.S. America*. I told him my two sisters and their families were on it—one coming from Pakistan and the other from the middle of Africa. My boss said okay. But I could see he thought it was such a good story he didn't know whether to believe it or not."

Mail was waiting for us at the Lutheran home for missionaries in New York. At the bottom of the pile we found a cablegram four days old. I read it quickly; my heart pounded as I then handed it silently to Walter. It had been sent from Leipzig when we were halfway across the Atlantic. It read:

"VATI DIED OF HEART ATTACK SATURDAY EVENING. MUTTI."

We opened a letter postmarked Leipzig. Most of it was in Vati's handwriting. In it he relived all the highspots of our visit, of our Christmas celebration together. It was filled with nostalgia for his children and his two grandchildren. Now there was only the empty crib, there was no little granddaughter to crawl up on his knee and play with his desk drawers; no little grandson with whom to pace the floor—only himself and Mutti. But he did not want us to think they were unhappy; they had much to keep them occupied. He had bought tickets so he could take Mutti to the play *Abraham Lincoln* next Wednesday. They would enjoy that. And on Saturday there would be a class reunion . . .

Those tickets for *Abraham Lincoln* were found unused in Vati's billfold. Wednesday was the day of his funeral.

A few minutes more and the Burlington Zephyr would be pulling into St. Paul. My fingers fumbled as I pulled on Kathy's snowsuit and bundled Danny up in all his blankets.

What would it be like to be reunited with my family again? Why, it would soon be ten years since I had seen little David and Mary starting out for Bolivia with Mother. Would I even know them if I saw them waiting? Let's see . . . David would be nineteen and Mary twenty-one.

The train stopped. From the platform a group seemed to be waving to us. Then I saw Mother, smiling through her tears. Beside her were Cliff and Lil Michelsen, whose furlough coincided with ours. But that fellow standing next to Mother, at least a towering six foot three . . . Why, that must be my baby brother David! And the sweet blond girl at his side . . . My sister Mary! Only the pain of separation could make the delight of home-coming so sweet.

As we drove up in front of a lovely house on Keston Street in St. Paul, Mother revealed that this would be our home. It had been assigned to us by the mission board for our furlough. Inside, we scarcely believed our eyes. There were carpeted floors, a modern kitchen, bath, and full basement—quite a contrast to Tchollire. I wanted to cry when we learned it had been furnished by the women of the church, down to the last dish towel. Even the cupboards and refrigerator had been stocked with food.

It was fun getting to know each other all over again, and greater fun still to discover the new members of our family. There were nieces and nephews, brothers and sisters by marriage, and new babies. Everyone blended into the family circle.

The far places of the world that were represented here! Borneo, for example. Only this time it wasn't the legendary wild man from Borneo, but a vivacious, warm, outgoing girl who had recently completed a term there as missionary teacher.

Six months ago she had been all set to go back and had already shipped her trunks. Her flight reservations were made for the end of August. Shortly before leaving she took part in a panel discussion on "Personal Adjustments of the Missionary" at a conference in St. Paul. She represented the well-adjusted single missionary girl.

Another member of the panel was a Dr. John Hult who was scheduled to leave soon for Tanganyika. Dr. Hult represented the medical side of missionary life.

There, across the conference table, the two met. It didn't take them long to discover that they had a few personal adjustments of their own to make.

Three years before, John had decided he must go to Tanganyika. He finished his residency in pediatrics in Denver soon after Louise's death. But then he discovered that he would need more experience both in surgery and in general practice. So he and Mother, with the three children, moved to the lumber town of Cloquet in northern Minnesota. There he worked side by side with our uncle, Dr. Einar Norberg, who had been with Father on the ill-fated *Zamzam*. John remained at Cloquet for two years, gaining invaluable experience.

At last the day came when he could inform the mission board

of his readiness to leave for the field.

Mother had promised to go with him to look after his children. But secretly she prayed it would not be necessary. Rather, she hoped that John might find the right girl who could be his wife and true comrade as well as mother to his three children.

After the missionary conference ended, John had a date one night with the girl from Borneo. Her departure was now less than a week away, and the mission board had already bought her ticket. John was not given to making quick decisions. But he made one that night. It was late when he called Mother and said:

"Mother, put the coffeepot on. I'll be home in a few minutes with Adeline. We've something to tell you."

When they arrived a few minutes later, they told her the news. Ad had agreed to change her name from Lundquist to Hult, and her destination from Borneo to Tanganyika. They were laughing and crying as all three embraced one another.

The wedding day was set within three weeks so Ad could go with John to Tulane University. The mission secretary, Dr. Burke, had given his approval. It was necessary to take a course in tropical medicine before leaving for Africa.

Everything went off beautifully, but it took a lot of paperwork to recover the trunks.

Walter and I had arrived home soon after the wedding. Our hearts were won immediately by this new sister of ours and we thanked God for her.

We were witnesses as she and John stood together in the front of the well-filled church in Cloquet to be commissioned as missionaries to Tanganyika.

We had a farewell dinner for them in our home before they left with the children: Margaret, now eight; Elly, six; and four-year-old Danny.

John was on his way back to the place where he was born, to the land of his dreams, to the country where he would also find his father's grave. There, also, he would see Veda.

One evening I went with my sister Mary to hear the Concordia College Choir at the great Central Lutheran Church in Minneapolis. The choir, which was nationally known, was under the direction of Paul Christiansen. The singers had just returned from their annual tour, which this year included concerts in both Carnegie Hall, New York, and Constitution Hall, Washington, D. C. Critics had praised them highly.

I sat in the crowded balcony next to one of the massive stone pillars and reveled in the music of these young voices. But I had eyes for only one of the blue-gowned singers, a tall, blond young man in the tenor section. Was it really possible that this was the same brother Gus whom I had last seen in Rock Island when he was only a high school freshman? The awful accident in which he almost lost his foot had happened only a few months afterward. I observed him carefully after the concert as he marched out with the others. There was only the slightest hint of a limp.

How can anyone not believe in miracles?

In Leipzig, Walter had shown me his childhood home and haunts. Now it was my turn to do the same. We planned a trip to the Homestead. We would go to Springfield by way of Moline to see Martha, my third sister, and get acquainted with her family.

Marty had been married to Max Wiemken two years earlier on our parents' wedding anniversary. We already knew the story of their romance, how after she had finished training at Moline Lutheran Hospital, Marty worked as a special nurse for a well-known bone surgeon. She also helped the doctor in the operating room. One day she saw her future husband for the first time—on the operating table. Later, the young patient visited the doctor's office for frequent checkups. With every whirlpool treatment prescribed, Max and Marty's romance grew.

At Moline Walter and I immediately felt the bond of kinship with this new brother of ours. Max was strong, hearty, genuine in his faith, and dependable. He worked for Bell Telephone Com-

pany and was fond of both pizza and golfing. They had a little
son, just a few months older than our Danny. The resemblance
between the two cousins was remarkable.

We next went to St. Louis and then to Springfield. It was May,
and the full bloom of spring was on the countryside. We could
understand how Father felt when he first succumbed to the
charms of the Ozarks. It would be hard to find any spot to rival
the quiet beauty and inviting restfulness of these Missouri hills.

Early on a warm evening we turned in to the familiar maple-
bordered lane. The air was sweet with the scent of wild crabapple
blossoms. Somewhere a mockingbird was singing. There were the
cobblestone houses, the rolling hills, all seemingly unchanged.

Then my eye caught something which had been added to the
landscape: a brand new building on a ridge to the westward, its
windows turned to gold by the setting sun. The new church!

Another dream of my father's finally realized! A lump came to
my throat as I thought of his earnest efforts to start a church in
the neighborhood.

The next day we went to look at the inside. Immediately I
sensed something out of the past. Then I recognized a familiar
object.

After the congregation of Father's church at Verona had
joined a larger one, the building was vacated and the pulpit given
to Father. It was the last pulpit from which he preached regularly. For years it had stood in a corner of our living room, a well-
loved piece of furniture.

Now here it was in the new church, a symbol of Father's pre-
vailing spirit!

It was a great satisfaction to see all that Pastor and Mrs. Carlson, together with the Homestead Board and friends and neighbors, had done during the ten years since Mother had given over
her home.

We stayed in the cottage which had been named Dar es Salaam
(Haven of Peace), and for us it was just that. Across the way was

Bethany Cottage, the old home of our childhood. The Carlsons lived there now, but soon they would be moving into a lovely new stone dwelling to the south of it.

We had come to the Homestead not only to rest, but to find the quietness in which to reach a decision about our future. We seemed to be in a period of inner emptiness. We tramped the hills and spent hours in quiet meditation, asking God to show us His way and plan.

Did He really want us to go back to Africa? We both knew that a call is not something that you have in your pocket for a lifetime. You have it only as long as the call calls.

Nearly every week we received letters from the congregation we had left behind. Many of the letter writers had been taught by us, and we knew well the effort it took to spell out a few simple lines. Here are some literal translations of what these boys wrote in Fulani:

Mana Zakariyou, one of the boys at Tchollire, to Walter: "I am sorry that you lost your father. But this is the dear God and we have not the right to quarrel with Him, who watches over us day and night and who has sent us into the world. . . . I like to be at the station. The pastor shows us the Word of God and Mr. Johnson gives us iron to make tools."

David Mbikoubou, the chauffeur for the French commandant: "The death of your father has moved me very much. But do not cry too much, for God has shown us that the earth is not our country. . . ."

Yaya: "I greet you together with your chidren and your wife. I greet everyone in Jesus' name. I heard the story that your father died. I thank God that He has received him well in heaven. Monsieur Ellingboe says that he would like to send me among the Durus to preach the Word of God. But it is God who sends me, not Monsieur."

Toma, our former cook: "After a little while my wife will give birth. There are still four months lacking. You must pray God for my wife every day that she may have strength. . . . I thank God that He changed my heart. I do not fall any more into temptation, because God has heard your prayers. . . . I grasp your hand in Jesus' name."

By the time we left the Homestead for St. Paul we had reached our decision. We again heard the strong call and commission. The words God had used to the prophet Ezekiel—"Son of man, I send you"—came to mind.

In the fall we would return to Africa.

School was out when Gus came to visit us, bringing his bride, Maria Mykannen. Her background was Finnish. She was a nurse, and continued in her profession in order that Gus might go on with his education.

Gus and Maria were hoping to be missionaries on the home front. Both of them were interested in serving among the American Indians. Maria had already spent some time as a nurse at the Red Lake Indian Reservation Hospital. They were confident that when Gus had finished his education, God would show them His place of service for them.

An exciting event was approaching—Mother's commissioning service—or perhaps I should say recommissioning service.

Now that John and his family had left for Tanganyika and Mother's hands were free, she was planning to return to Bolivia. She was fifty-eight, in good health, and she saw no reasons, other than selfish ones, not to go. She was needed there. So quietly, she began to get ready.

On a warm Sunday evening in July we all gathered at Trinity Church of Minnehaha Falls in Minneapolis, the church that had played such an important part in my life. Present were Max and Martha, Gus and Maria, Vince and Eunie, David and Mary, and Walter and I. Gus sang "Lost in the Night," Eunie and Vince, a duet on the 67th Psalm. Walter delivered the message.

Mother, in giving her greeting, reminded us that when she left for Bolivia the first time ten years before, she had just become a grandmother. Now she was fourteen times a grandmother. But she did not consider it any reason to stay at home. I heard once more the echo of her words uttered on that other day so long ago: "This business of carrying the Gospel to all the world is so important that even we grandmothers have to go!"

When Mother was ready to leave, she wrote to Paul, who was station manager for Frontier Airlines in Tucson, and asked him if he could get her a pass to Miami. She had been working as librarian in the nursing school at Deaconess Hospital in Minneapolis since John left and saved enough to pay for her plane ticket from Miami to La Paz. Paul sent the pass.

She woke up about five-thirty one morning and called the airport as she had been doing. This time she learned that a plane was leaving at seven and had an empty seat. Her suitcase was packed. The coffeepot was on. There was time only for a cup together and then we hurried to the airport. I was disappointed that she hadn't even allowed her children the chance to give her a farewell dinner. But that was the way she wanted it.

Out at the Wold-Chamberlain field it was gray and chilly. The raw wind whipped our coats and scarves. Mother checked her well-worn suitcase. It came under the forty-four-pound limit. This was her only baggage. After one last embrace for each of her children, she smiled at us and consoled us by saying:

"Let's not be saddened by the pain of separation. We must be faithful the short while we live. Remember what we have to look forward to: all eternity to spend together."

Briskly, she mounted the steps of the small plane that would take her to Chicago. She hoped to make connections the same day for New York to see Carl. She would go on to Washington, D.C., where Roy, her oldest brother, lived, and then down to Miami.

She took a seat by the window and waved to us as the landing steps were rolled away and the engines started up. I got a quick glimpse of her face, its gentle strength framed with white hair.

I remembered something Walter had said after our wedding, when Mother bade us good-by as we were about to be separated by oceans:

"Ingrid, your mother is great!"

Great, yes; that was the word for it, although she would be the last to agree.

Fourteen.

Two Dauntless Grandmothers

A month after Mother left for Bolivia, Walter and I packed our belongings, and with our two babies, began the long trip by train, boat, and plane back to Africa.

We were not returning to Tchollire, now ably cared for by Pastor and Mrs. Ellingboe and by Ernie and Helen Johnson. Instead, we were assigned to Cameroun Christian College in Libamba, the school we visited on our first trip to Africa. It was sponsored by the Protestant missions to provide higher education for the most promising young people. Walter would teach German and Bible, and also serve as a campus pastor.

Libamba was quite different from Tchollire. Here was the virgin forest—*"le prison vert"* ("the green prison"), the French called it—with the mighty crowns of its giant trees interlacing to block out the sky. The jungle was all around us, an impenetrable wall hiding dark secrets.

Dampness was our enemy. It often rained for days on end; the rainfall averaged fourteen feet a year.

We had to insert a layer of waxed paper under the flap of every unused envelope and between new postage stamps. We rubbed soap on the drawers to keep them from sticking. Our shoes turned green with mold if we didn't wear them every day; our clothing mildewed on the hangers. Salt left in an open dish turned into water overnight. Even our pillows never lost their musty, tropical smell.

Our work here also contrasted greatly with what we had done in Tchollire. There we had spent our first term working in a completely unevangelized territory. We had to be creative, to explore new land, for there were no beaten tracks. There, too, we had to teach people to read and write. Here at Libamba these students of ours would one day become the educated "elite" of an important emerging country: the future teachers, lawyers, doctors, and pastors—yes, political leaders, too. Many of them would continue their studies at European or American universities.

We had no illusions, however. We were aware that most were not here to become Christians, nor to serve the Kingdom of God by what they learned.

Long before our first year was over and we got to know the students as individuals, we realized the challenge ahead of reaching these intelligent young Africans with the power of Jesus Christ, whose message is not to rule, but to serve.

As for ourselves, instead of living in isolation we were now members of an international faculty. We welcomed the opportunity to exchange viewpoints and ideas.

Our home this time was not made of mud, but of metal.

Ten years ago the college had purchased a number of prefabricated iron huts to be used as temporary housing for the faculty. They were still in service. Having been used by the U.S. Army in North Africa as hospital wards for mental patients, they had a number of unusual features.

Ours stood on stilts to keep out the moisture. Inside, everything was metal except for the plywood floors and plywood doors. The doors had been equipped with glass peepholes for the purpose of observing the behavior of the occupants. (They proved very useful in keeping an eye on our children.) The ceilings were low and consisted of a heavy metal screen: Any conversation at one end of the house could easily be overheard at the other end.

One of the more pleasant features was a long covered veranda in the back where the children could play and where the washing could be hung up to dry in rainy weather.

It was a strange structure to convert into a home. Yet it was precisely that project which had challenged me on arrival. I began with the windows—only screen-covered openings. In the native market I found a bolt of material with a green-and-brown design which just suited my fancy. Out of that I made curtains for the bedrooms. For the living-room drapes I dyed a large piece of homespun material which had been woven in Rey Bouba, lined it, and hung it up. We used the mats the Lamido had given us to decorate the walls. Then we hung up the cuckoo clock, as well as the brass gong which had been our first church bell at Tchollire.

I found wooden crates, painted them, and put them in the children's room for their toys. Bamboo shades went up in Walter's office. More crates served as bookshelves.

One of our friends wrote to us exuberantly, telling of her new apartment in California "furnished in Danish modern with Oriental accessories." Walter replied to her note that our new home was furnished in "Presbyterian ancient [the furniture had been fashioned a number of decades earlier at the Presbyterian Mission Industrial School] with African accessories."

But we were happy in this home. For the next six years it would be for us an island of peace in the midst of all the storms surrounding us.

At Libamba, too, we had to become accustomed to a new set of unfamiliar noises. We no longer listened for the trampling feet of elephants as they uprooted small trees close to our house. Rather, we waited twice each day for the huffing of the train and its sharp whistle as it chugged along a quarter of a mile away, between the port city of Douala and the capital, Yaounde. Or the loud purring of the Diesel generator which furnished electricity every evening from six to ten in the study halls and in the teachers' homes . . . Or the *knock-knock* of the gasoline pump as it drew water from the river to supply our needs . . . Or the noisy, persistent Caterpillar as it busily built roads, nosing over trees and leveling ground to make a beautiful campus out of virgin forest . . .

One morning we found in our mailbox a letter addressed in Mother's familiar handwriting. But this time it was postmarked Apolo, Bolivia, instead of La Paz. Did that mean she was no longer at the orphanage or at the mission home where she had served her first term? I tore open the envelope and read:

"As you see, my new address is Apolo. It's a lonely station nestled in the foothills of the eastern slope of the Andes mountains with an altitude of five thousand feet (that's seven thousand feet lower than La Paz, where I was last term). Melba Kittelsen, just your age, Ingrid, is stationed here with me, so we're quite a team. I tell her she's the 'Pa' and I'm the 'Ma.' She does the preaching at our weekly services while I play the organ and direct the singing. She's in charge of the workmen (who are building a mule shed for us right now), while I take care of the household.

"Our only means of communication with the outside world is through the weekly mail plane from La Paz, but when the weather isn't just right here in the mountains, even that doesn't function.

"Last week Melba and I made our first mule trip to Tananpaya. It's one of the stations on the other side of the mountain ridge where we have a school and a small group of believers whom we try to visit once a month. Each trip is a three-day expedition. I was a little afraid at first, for it's been several years now since I was on a mule on the mountain trail, but I soon got over it. I had a bit of a cold when we left, but with the sun, sweat, and exercise I quickly lost that. Through the walking and being shaken on the mule as we go down steep places, I lost a little weight too, but that's good for me. . . .

"Thanks so much for the bit of Danny's hair after his first

haircut. The tangible, soft, silky tresses of a dear little boy made me cry. I'm so glad I have pictures of all of you. They're lined up on my dressing table, which is made out of the wooden boxes we get kerosene in. With a long plyboard top and a skirt of blue underneath, it serves even as a place for my books. . . . "

Walter and I sat reading her letter aloud. How characteristic of her, I thought, to be jogging on a mule over rugged mountain trails and thinking nothing of it, even with her sixtieth birthday only a few months away.

Suddenly her letter reminded me of her first trip to Bolivia. She had landed safely in La Paz. At that time the only way to get from the motor road to Coaba Farm, where the orphanage was located, was either by walking or by riding muleback for more than three miles.

The mission in La Paz sent a telegram to Coaba Farm, asking that three or four mules be at the motor road the next day to meet Mother and her co-worker, Violet Anderson.

Somehow the message became confused. The good people at the farm were somewhat mystified when they were requested to have forty mules on hand to meet Mrs. Hult. The mission staff set out in all directions to recruit every available mule. Mother wasn't sure she was going to ride a mule at all down the steep mountain path. One can only imagine her amazement when she found more than thirty of the beasts awaiting her!

Her zest for life—she was always ready for the most strenuous undertakings—together with her interest in people soon endeared her to everyone. Before long she had a new name. Not only the orphans, but the Indians, the nationals, and her co-workers, were all calling her *"Mamita"* ("Little Mother"). The mission director had told me once: "The most remarkable thing about your mother is her ability to fit in anywhere."

And that's exactly what Mother had to do during her years in Bolivia. She served first as "mother" at the orphanage; later as teacher in the orphanage school where she taught Spanish to the third, fourth, fifth, and sixth grades.

Our routine was interrupted one day by a happy surprise. Veda, who had been in the States on her first furlough, wrote that she was coming to visit us on her way back to Tanganyika.

Eagerly, we prepared for her arrival. Walter would stay home with Danny, now eighteen months, while Kathy, almost three, and I went by train the fifty miles to Yaounde to meet Veda at the airport.

At Yaounde, we spent the night with friends. The following morning we went out to the airport just in time to see the plane from Douala come in for a landing. I strained my eyes for my first glimpse of Veda. The passengers straggled down the runway, but she wasn't among them.

I was mystified. Upon inquiry, I found that her flight from Paris had been delayed and thus missed connections with this plane. It would be necessary to wait another twenty-four hours for the next one.

We were on hand again to meet it in the morning. Still no Veda! By this time I was really worried. All night I had the feeling that something must have happened to her. I even had a terrifying nightmare that she was dying.

I heard the inter-com calling me to the desk. There was a message for me: "Mademoiselle Hult was unable to board the plane this morning because of a severe nasal hemorrhage. She has been hospitalized in Douala."

My poor sister! To have this happen to her when she was traveling all alone in a strange land! Then I remembered that she did not know a word of French. I wasn't quite sure what I should do. I wanted to go to her. But I was expecting our third child within a few weeks and knew I ought not to make the long trip to Douala by train.

It so happened that one of the teachers was in Yaounde; Kathy and I had a chance to ride with him back to Libamba if we left right away. I accepted. Once home, Walter and I talked it over and decided that he must take the night train to Douala to help his stricken sister-in-law. He rode all night in the crowded third-class car, where he had the choice of either standing in the aisle or sitting on his suitcase. But he arrived safely the next morning in Douala.

Here is Veda's story as she wrote it in her diary:

"During the overnight flight from Paris to Douala I began having nosebleeds. And that night, alone in a Douala hotel, I ended up with a bad nasal hemorrhage. There was nothing I could do to stop it. I called for help. There was quite a commotion in the hotel before a doctor came and I was on the way to the hospital. As I realized I was losing consciousness, these thoughts passed through my mind: 'I'm in Africa now, not in Minneapolis General where they have a blood bank, but . . . I am completely safe . . . I am in His keeping . . . I'm ready to die . . .'

"Don't know when I've been so glad to see anyone as the morning Walter walked into my hospital room in Douala. For the first time I could talk to my French doctor—through an interpreter. (I had other ideas as to the best way of getting back my strength than the r-a-r-e meat and wine I was being served.)

"Air travel was out in my present condition. But with Walter's help I was able to continue by train to Libamba where I met Ingrid, Kathy, and Danny.

"What was only going to be a two-week stay in Cameroun turned out to be two months. It took that long before I was back to normal physically and had the doctor's permission to continue travel by air. And because of the delay I had the privilege of being on hand to welcome my new nephew, David Johannes Trobisch, on August 18."

And it was a privilege for me to have my own sister as private-duty nurse after David's birth. Both David and I thrived on her loving care. The time for her to leave for Tanganyika came all too soon. It took her two weeks to cross the continent by plane, owing to unexpected delays in Yaounde, Leopoldville, and Usumbura. At the end of the trip, however, was a happy reunion with John and Ad and their family.

They had finished their Swahili language study in Tanganyika, and John was absorbed in his medical work. For a few short weeks Veda and John would be working together there before John moved to another station.

It was always good to hear from John and to learn of his experiences as a missionary doctor. He was serving in an area very close to where Dr. Paul White, author of the "Jungle Doctor" books, had worked. In one of his letters John wrote:

"Until the return of Dr. Stanley Moris, whom I am temporarily replacing, I am responsible for the work at the leprosarium near Iambi. What a challenge! In our whole area there are about ten thousand patients with the disease, less than a thousand of whom are being treated. With the help of the American Leprosy Mission we are building a new treatment center and colony which will take care of five hundred or more patients. We have already moved about eighty of the least disabled to help with the building and cultivation. This brings new responsibilities for the doctor, not always medical.

"In September, the small herd of cattle were getting ill. After one or two died, we discovered they had sleeping sickness. Since there were no vets around, it fell to me to do something about it. I had no trouble in getting the proper drug, but to administer it, I had only the puny little syringes and needles we use for humankind.

"Gathering all our paraphernalia together, my helpers and I bravely entered the arena, a big long corral. It had the makings of a real rodeo. A crowd gathered on the top rails to cheer us on.

"The cattle—big bruisers closely related to the wild Brahmans used in rodeos back home—weren't particularly interested in submitting to the treatment of the quack 'horse doctor.' One of the leprosy patients who had only stumps for hands was quite skillful in lassoing the brutes. But he wasn't satisfied at going for their heads; he had to get them by one front leg. Then about ten other patients, in various stages of deformity, grabbed ahold of the loose ends and were slung around the corral a few times until the beast slowed down a bit.

"Then they yelled at me in Swahili: 'Okay, Doc, do your stuff.' As soon as I approached the animal, he'd make a few more turns about the arena. Then I'd sneak up as close as possible and make a wild stab at the closest part of the anatomy. As often as not, the needle would break or bend double and we'd start all over again. After about two hours the job was done and a great cheer arose from the assembled crowd. Actually, though, it wasn't so much worse than some of the tussles I've had with little boys in a certain pediatric office back in Minnesota. Furthermore, we are happy to report all the patients recovered."

I'm sure John never thought he'd be a cow doctor when he decided to go to Tanganyika—but still more unforeseen experiences would lie ahead for him.

We could hardly claim that our children were born with silver spoons in their mouths, but we did have two very unusual grandmothers to offer them. While Mother was riding her mules in Bolivia, Mutti, at sixty-five, was getting ready to set forth on an adventure of her own.

Since she was now alone in Leipzig after Vati's death, we had invited her to join us at Libamba. She asked the Communist authorities for an exit visa. Her request was turned down under the pretext that the East German government had to protect its citizens from the atomic fallout to which they would be exposed on the western side of the Iron Curtain. Undaunted, she made still another request, using the argument that her third grandchild would be born in August and she wanted to be there to help.

But an official replied with an indifferent shrug:

"Millions of babies have been born in this world without you. Application denied."

Mutti made up her mind to leave without a visa. She had a friend in the American Sector of West Berlin. Packing her old brown suitcase with her most precious possessions, she proceeded to travel by train from Leipzig to East Berlin. At the station she checked her suitcase, taking out only a few things to put in her black marketing bag, which was carried by every German house-wife. With this in her hand she passed the control officer at the subway and went by subway across the Iron Curtain to the home of her friend without arousing suspicion. Eight times she repeated this risky journey on different days and at various hours, leaving her things each time at her friend's home.

Mutti went back to Leipzig for the last time. She waited for a coded telegram from her friend. The message would tell her that we had sent the plane ticket and the flight date. At last it came:

"THE WEDDING WILL BE ON AUGUST 14 STOP WEAR YOUR YELLOW DRESS."

On Sunday Mutti attended services in the Thomaskirche in Leipzig. As she heard the text for the day from Luke 9:62, "No one who puts his hand to the plow and looks back, is fit for the kingdom of God," it spoke to her heart. Her decision had been reaffirmed.

The next day Mutti, dressed in a rust-colored wool suit (one that Walter had sent her from America), without a hat to cover her carefully waved silver-gray hair, and carrying only a small overnight bag, closed the door of her apartment behind her.

She boarded the streetcar and went out to the city cemetery, where she visited the graves of her beloved husband and only daughter. A moment of silence, and then she turned resolutely away. Her train would leave from the downtown central station in half an hour.

She was slightly nervous as she bought her ticket to East Berlin and hurriedly boarded the train. She was thankful that her com-partment was empty; no one would see her tears. Never had she felt so completely alone, for she dared tell none of her friends of her plans. It could get them into serious trouble with the State. She was leaving behind forever her home, her friends, the graves of her loved ones, and the city where she had been born and where she had lived her life.

In East Berlin she composed herself to face the last barrier, the customs control at the subway entrance. The officer asked for her passport. He stamped it. He asked her to open her suitcase—nothing in it except her toilet articles and overnight things. He silently waved her on.

Two days later Mutti arrived safely by plane in Yaounde where Walter met her.

We had a touching reunion. She came at a busy time. Four days later her second grandson, David, was born.

One evening Mutti confided to us that once as a young girl she had almost become engaged to a missionary in Africa. (He had been living on the slopes of Kilimanjaro at the same station where I was born.) He had written his letter of proposal from Africa, and just as he was about to mail it, the announcement of her betrothal to Vati reached him. "But I always had a feeling that someday I would get to Africa," she said to us. "And now this is the crowning event of my life."

Although Mutti had never before been in a foreign country, she adjusted admirably. More that forty years had passed since she studied both English and French at a private school in Leipzig. But now both languages came back to her. She spoke them fluently. Mutti had taught for ten years before her marriage. Since Libamba was always in need of more teachers, she was asked by the director to take over the beginning classes in German.

So, in addition to her grandmotherly occupations, she also taught side by side with Walter. Some of her students were a head taller than she, yet they gave her no trouble, for the Africans have deep respect for age. In fact, the students closest to her soon asked permission to call her Mama.

During Veda's visit with us, she had told us the surprising but happy news about Carl. He had accepted a position as a representative of Lutheran World Relief in the Far East and would be leaving for Korea in the fall.

Veda had also brought us up to date on the other members of the family. Mary was in her last year of nurse's training at Swed-

ish Hospital in Minneapolis. David was working as an orderly at
Fairview Hospital there while he continued his courses at the
University of Minnesota. Gus and Maria were in Florida, working together in an old people's home which Maria's father had
founded; Gus was preparing to graduate from Stetson University
at Deland. Eunie and Vince, with their four children, were living
near Rock Island where Vince served as pastor for two Methodist
congregations while pursuing his theological studies at Augustana
Seminary. They looked forward to the day when they might again
return to Pakistan. Max and Martha were nearby in Moline with
their family, and Paul and Ann were in Tucson.

In my thankfulness I thought once more of the first Psalm
which my father had quoted so often to us, and which his father
had given him:

> Blessed is the man . . . whose delight is in the law of the Lord . . .
> And he shall be like a tree planted by the streams of water,
> That bringeth forth its fruit in its season. . . .

"Like a tree"—a tree whose branches were reaching out, not
only to the east, west, north, and south of our own country, but
into the other continents as well.

Fifteen.

Seedtime at Libamba

A gathering cloud now cast a shadow over our pleasant life in Libamba as pressure for independence mounted in French Cameroun. The extreme nationalists, the *maquisards*, were outlawed by the government. They then went into hiding in the forest, coming out at night to spread terror by killing and kidnaping.

The African district chief ordered a seven o'clock curfew, announcing that anyone caught outside after that hour would be shot on sight by his soldiers.

One night we were kept awake by gunfire nearby. The campus became an armed camp. In the morning government soldiers stomped through our house, and we learned there had been a fight in the forest. A wounded *maquisard* had escaped and the French army captain, thinking he might have sought shelter in one of the homes of the faculty, had ordered all our houses searched. No trace of the man was found.

The students reflected the unrest. They were given to sudden, unaccountable acts, such as classroom and hunger strikes, violence against one another, even disrespect for teachers. The most patient counseling could neither prevail upon them nor disclose any rational motive for their moves.

The national situation was explosive. Independence had to come. We knew that. But what would be our role as teachers? The future was at best obscure, and also dangerous.

Word reached us that elsewhere in Cameroun, missionaries facing similar circumstances had been forced to flee for their lives. We were worried over the safety of the children. We made ready to leave on a moment's notice—and waited.

I was also concerned about Walter.-He grew paler and thinner day by day. Recurring attacks of malaria, the unfriendly climate, and a heavy schedule were taking their toll. Besides a full teaching load, he had also made himself available to students as counseling pastor at all hours.

Worst of all was the mounting frustration in our work as missionaries. As we expressed it in a letter to friends at the time:

"It isn't the muggy climate, nor the snakes, nor the baby mice in the shower pail. It isn't even the lack of strawberries with whipped cream, or as some may think, the fact that we are bored because we have no television.

"It is rather that sometimes we feel that not only are we not fulfilling the Great Commission, we are actually working against it."

Why did we feel this way? Was it because few of our students regarded attendance at a Christian college as an opportunity for spiritual growth and enlightenment? We knew they looked upon the tuition for which their parents had made great sacrifices as an investment which would pay dividends when the students got lucrative positions because of their education.

We did have some, however, who expressed their desire to take a stand for Christ. Our experiences with them were inspiring, as when Walter was invited to conduct a three-day retreat for mission high school students at Metet, a village about sixty miles away.

Walter wanted his Libamba college boys to undertake most of the program. He formed a team. The boys rehearsed for weeks,

meeting every Sunday morning for at least an hour before breakfast. It was the only free time in their busy student schedules.
They questioned anything on the program that was not clear and
laughed at anything that Africans might find misleading. Finally
one day they all got on a bus and went to Metet.

The theme chosen was "The Effectiveness of Magic." Walter
opened the program. The hundred young high school students
listened intently to his introductory remarks. Then the Libamba
team took over. A boy named Justin spoke first. He was somewhat ill at ease in the large room as he talked to boys almost his
own age.

He told them of his fear of superstition and of how he had been
freed once he put God in first place. Then his cousin Emmanuel,
strong, broad-shouldered, the son of a chief, described his own
battle. The other boys on the team—Jean, Simeon, Joseph, and
Thomas—each spoke in turn with a down-to-earth illustration of
how he had been set free from the grip of superstition, sorcery,
and fortunetelling.

During the meeting the listeners stirred uneasily. At the close,
all was quiet. The students filed out soberly. Walter had no doubt
that the messages struck home.

In fact, many of the Metet high school boys afterward saw
Walter privately. They declared their intention of giving up their
old ways to follow Christ. As evidence of their seriousness, they
handed over their charms and fetishes.

To his surprise, Walter found that these objects were not African in origin. Mostly, they had been ordered from either Europe
or America, and undoubtedly at enormous expense to these poor
youths.

He examined the fetishes. Among them were "magic" fountain
pens that would enable the owners to pass any examination;
"magic" medals that would give them skill in mathematics (always one of the most difficult subjects for these young Africans);
a wide variety of "magic" rings and handkerchiefs; and a "magic"
perfume that had the power of winning a girl's love.

Walter's discovery prompted him to further questioning. He learned that almost half of the high school students were corresponding regularly with some astrologer or "professor of magic" in Tangier, Nice, Paris, New York, or Chicago, and receiving advice. Walter was filled with indignation at the cynical way in which these trusting youngsters were being exploited.

Out of this retreat came further invitations: From time to time the Libamba team would visit other schools in the area. We took new heart in our work.

Shortly after Walter's return from Metet we found a telegram in our mailbox. It was from our mission director at Poli. I opened it with trembling hands. "HELEN JOHNSON"—these were the first words I saw.

Helen had died two days ago at Tchollire. I was stunned. I couldn't believe it—not Helen, whose striking outer beauty was illumined by an inner beauty of loving unselfishness . . . Helen, who had come to Tchollire as a bride three years ago . . . Helen, who, working side by side with me that last year at Tchollire, was as dear to me as one of my own sisters . . . In her last letter she had told me how happy they were as they planned their first furlough. They would stop in Norway to see relatives, and then go on home to Seattle . . .

I found my way to our bedroom where I could close the door and be alone. I sat down at my desk and buried my head in my arms. My thoughts went back to the time when Helen and Ernie had arrived at Tchollire late one afternoon, tired, hot, and dusty, their truck loaded to the falling-off point.

I recalled the day when she first came to work at the dispensary, all crisp and fresh in her new uniform. How would she, trained in a modern hospital and accustomed to following a doctor's orders, adjust to primitive conditions where she would have to treat patients on her own, with the mission doctor expected only once every two or three months? For a clinic we had only a round mud hut equipped with two packing-box cupboards and a straw bed. She met the challenge.

I could see her now, her long blond hair falling down around her face as she sawed and nailed boards to make a badly needed combination table and shelves; or as she cared for a sick African baby with as much love as if it had been her own; or as she patiently repeated a lesson for her class of boys from seven to sixteen, most of whom had scarcely seen a book and had never held a pencil in their hands.

I remembered, too, the moonlit evening when Walter and I sat in front of our house for a few minutes of quiet after a busy day. Strains of music came to our ears . . . the haunting melody of *Solveig's Song* by Grieg. To hear for the first time the music of Helen's violin in the stillness of the African night . . . On other evenings we could hear her clear soprano blending in with Ernie's tenor to the accompaniment of the harmonium, a present from the home church. In the isolation of our lonely outpost, this music was like a ray from heaven . . .

And now God had taken her. I thought of Psalm 48:14, which Helen once had told me was their wedding verse: "For this God is our God for ever and ever: He will be our guide even unto death."

We learned from the letter which followed the telegram that Helen and Ernie said these words together, and that they were her last. She had been sick only a few hours, suffering from what appeared to be a ruptured tubal pregnancy. To reach a doctor would have entailed seven hours of hard travel. She knew she was dying and said to Ernie: "I want to pass quickly." They had devotions together. "I can't pray out loud," she told him. Then she whispered the words of the psalm. A few minutes later, just before midnight, she died in his arms in the grass-roofed room that had been their first home in Africa—and also ours.

Except for his African companions, Ernie was alone on the station. The Ellingboes had been transferred to Meiganga. The nearest missionaries were at Poli, three hours away by truck. He sent them a message, asking: "Can someone come and bury

Helen?" It was noon the next day before Don and Grace Flatten reached Tchollire. Don conducted the funeral service. Then Helen was buried beside the dispensary. There her grave would bespeak a sermon mightier than words.

During our summer vacation that year we made a trip back to Tchollire. Ernie had left; at the moment no missionaries lived at the station.

But we were pleased to see that the African Christians were meeting the test. Where we had worked so hard to plant the seed, we found a healthy, self-supporting, indigenous church. Two catechists carried on the pastoral duties; elders had been elected; preaching places had been organized in several villages nearby. The treasurer at Tchollire kept the weekly offerings in a big fifty-gallon gasoline barrel filled with stones and padlocked for safe-keeping.

We thought of the words of Paul in I Corinthians 3:6: "I planted, Apollos watered, but God gave the growth."

We visited Helen's grave, marked with a simple wooden cross. As we meditated, heads bowed, Toma came and stood beside us in silence. After a moment he said:

"You come and go. All the other missionaries come and go. But Madame Johnson stays with us always."

Early in September, 1959, in our third school year at Libamba, a long letter came from John in Tanganyika. For several months after his co-director left on furlough, he had been in sole charge of the hundred-bed hospital at Kiomboi. It was a heavy burden for one doctor. He and his staff also treated nearly four hundred outpatients every day. Without the help of well-trained African medical assistants and the staff of devoted American missionary nurses, he could never have managed it.

John wrote:

"Just to give you a little idea of what goes into a day's work here at Kiomboi: Today I repaired a harelip, removed a cataract, and did two major surgeries, all of which, in the States, I would have referred to specialists. After I got out of surgery, I found a child with a broken leg waiting for me. Since I am not only the doctor, but also the only local X-ray technician, I took a picture and then put the little guy up in traction.

"Then the police came along with a murder case, and wanted an autopsy. Outside my office the usual number of 'routine' patients were waiting. I found it difficult at first to tackle the cases I didn't feel qualified to handle. But when people beg you to help them and there's nobody else—what do you do? Take those who were waiting. I'm sure that the situation of each has been improved (except the one that required the autopsy!). My biggest frustration is in not being able to do more pediatrics and more real public health.

"One of our most interesting patients was a medicine man or 'witchdoctor' who had tuberculosis. When he came to Kiomboi he was in bad shape. He had tried all of his own remedies to no avail. I put him on our medicine. Within six months he had gained thirty pounds and had stopped coughing.

"He was quite impressed and asked if I couldn't teach him. In turn, he offered to share *his* lore with me. I explained to him that it would be a bit difficult, since he could neither read nor write. Thereupon he asked for books. He really worked at it for a few days. But then finally he decided he'd better stick to his way. After all, on his own he could get a patient to give him a cow for a cure, whereas at the hospital we charge only a few shillings.

"I gave him one of my doctor's coats. You should have seen him beam when he put it on. When I saw him last week, it looked as though he hadn't had it off in three months. These witchdoctors are actually quite shrewd and some of their medications do have value. But they have no concept of dosage. If a little medicine is good, why shouldn't a whole gourdful be that much better? If the patient dies after his treatment, well, that's bad luck. The government has outlawed their practice, but the people still go to them, and when the witchdoctors are in trouble, they refuse to testify against them."

As I put down John's letter, I felt a strong surge of pride mingled with love for this brother who had been my closest companion in childhood. His compassion for the suffering, which had endeared him to us even as children, must be felt also by his African brethren.

I got to thinking of family love. Are we to be ashamed of it or try to hide it? I remembered an incident soon after my father's death, when the family had moved from Springfield to Wahoo, and Veda, Eunie, Carl, and I were all students at the Academy. We often met between classes. One of my classmates said to me one day:

"What's the matter with you Hults? You see some member of your family in the hall, or on the stairs, your faces just light up and you greet each other as if—well, just as if you loved each other. I can't figure it out."

"Maybe that's what's the matter with us," I replied. "We do love each other."

And because of this love overflowing among us, there was love to share with others. I could sense it, too, in Carl's early letters from Korea. He told of his first impressions:

"Korea is certainly a disjointed country. When you consider that these people spent forty years under the Japanese, another five years as an independent, though divided, nation, and then went through a terrible war, it is easy to understand why. It is terribly overcrowded because of the influx of refugees from North Korea. There's little chance for economic independence because almost all the industry—the electrical generating plants included—is located in the north.

"I spent the first three weeks here in Seoul in the main office of the Korean Church World Service, getting acquainted with the projects in this area, and also making a tour of the provinces in the south.

"Pusan is the major Korean port. No matter how you look at it, the city is an enigma. According to all the rules of logic, it should be a city without hope. Here we have over a million people, more than half of whom are either seriously underemployed or completely unemployed. It is not rare to see a family of six or seven living in a box-type house, seven feet by seven feet, constructed from scrap lumber, pieces of canvas, packing cases, cardboard, and tin cans. Hundreds of these houses are located on the edge of some downtown street. Other thousands of them are located row on row, in stairstep fashion, on the steep hillsides surrounding the harbor area.

"Yet in spite of all the poverty and disease, the people still go about their daily tasks with hope. Hundreds of children leave for school each morning with a determined countenance and purposeful tread, even though they are too poor to afford any lunch, and will have only a meager dinner in the evening. The man who makes deliveries with a small, two-wheeled cart or by carrying loads on his own back, trudges on, day after day, in the expectation that tomorrow, or next week, or next year, will bring him a better job."

Carl said the relief work was doing much to encourage and undergird this hope. Fifteen feeding stations scattered over the city made it possible for thousands to have a hot meal every day. Three stations were also useful in implementing the distribution of clothing and food for hospitals and orphanages.

"With the fifty million pounds of relief supplies which Korean Church World Service has been bringing in each year, it's a pretty big job which I have to arrange storage and inland shipment for the incoming goods. We have a very good Korean staff here—about twenty people. It's a wonderful challenge to gain their confidence and to try to teach them some of our Western ways of doing things. . . .

"On the other hand, I was soon aware of a culture which is older than Western civilization. Often when I am in the presence of a well-educated Korean, I think how clumsy we are. To see the graceful and restrained movements and gestures, to hear the smoothness of speech, and to be welcomed in their polite way, sometimes gives this ungraceful American an inferiority complex.

"I don't know exactly how to say it, but it is good to come home at the end of a long day and feel that because of your efforts, some people, who would not otherwise have eaten, will be able to have a meal this evening."

A picture flashed to my mind when I read the last sentence. It was back on the Homestead in Missouri during our childhood days. We had a deep well there which supplied us with clear, sparkling cold water.

But in order to get the water you had to pump it. And that was serious business. We so much admired our father, or Paul and John, who, with long, even strokes of the pump handle, could fill the water pail in short order. One by one, as we grew up, each of us was trained to pump. First we would only hang on while we helped someone older and stronger. At last the moment came when we were allowed to try it alone. We would give a little jump and then, pressing with all our might, bring the handle down a few inches. More tries—and finally the reward of a trickle of water. When you could fill a bucket in this way, it was evidence that you were grown up.

I remember the day when this happened to Carl. We ran to our parents, crying out:

"Carl has grown up! Carl has grown up! He can pump a pail of water all by himself!" And there on the pump stand beside his full bucket was five-year-old Carl, grinning from ear to ear, sweat trickling down his brow, as triumphant as if he had just climbed Mt. Everest.

I now thought of the boy pumping fresh, cool water for his thirsty family. And I also thought of the man ministering to those in desperate need, and in this way witnessing to the sustaining love of Christ. Wasn't the one a symbol of the other?

In another letter Carl described a village he had visited in the Chiri Mountains, where thirty-five families eked out a living by farming small patches on the steep slopes:

"The physical environment is beautiful. The tall, rocky mountains, dotted with bamboo groves and scrub pine, reach toward the sky. Clear mountain streams rush down valleys and ravines. But here the beauty ends. One glance into the faces of the people betrays their grinding poverty.

"Here is a forty-year-old farmer whose drawn cheeks, wrinkled brow, and haunted, suspicious eyes reveal years of backbreaking labor, of long periods when there was only enough food to keep alive, of no education, and of the continuous worry of being unable to provide for his family.

"Here is a five-year-old boy whose pallid skin, pinched face, and listless eyes tell of a home where even the bare necessities of life were not always available.

"And over here is an old grandmother whose tattered, dirty clothing and anxiety-pinched face bespeak a lifetime spent clinging to the fringes of existence.

"The Korean farmer has three acres of land on which he is able to produce barely enough to feed himself and his family. To put it more graphically, from the same amount of land needed by one American farmer, thirty Korean families derive their livelihood."

Carl hoped to find more constructive ways than distributing relief supplies to help the chronically poor in rural areas.

He soon found an opportunity for direct action in an undertaking known as the Dae Duk project. A thousand families, nearly all refugees from North Korea, and destitute, were living in hovels on a plain by the sea. They had no resources, no funds, no hope for the future, indeed, no place in the new land. Then a young North Korean engineer, Mr. Kim, got the idea of reclaiming land from the Yellow Sea. The refugees went to work. With their own hands they undertook to construct a dam which, when finished, would make available three thousand acres of new fertile land. When Carl heard of this he was so impressed that he made the project his own deep concern. Later he would receive a letter of commendation from the South Korean government for his part in procuring the materials necessary for building the dam.

Pastor Ove Nielsen, an official of Lutheran World Relief, described the project graphically after Carl took him on a tour of the work:

"I felt a sense of deep admiration and respect as I heard dynamite explode and saw stubborn rock blasted from the hillsides. After each series of blasts, throngs of men, women, and children scurried forth to gather up the pieces and deposit them in the mining cars. Then the cars were pushed by men out onto the farthest reach of the dam and the contents dumped into the Yellow Sea.

"Faces of the workers reflected pride in their achievement. The workers were obviously being driven by a sense of common purpose. Many were clad in rags and were underfed, but they were not people to be pitied. . . ."

Pastor Nielsen turned to Carl as he watched them and said:

"I have just *seen* a sermon."

Later, upon his return to the States on furlough, Carl, looking back on his experiences in Korea, wrote this:

"It has been a blessing to me and has added richness to my life. I know of no better way to show others our faith than to work in ministering to those who are hungry and homeless."

I thought again about my picture of him as a boy and of its significance: not a cupful but a bucketful.

Through many personal conversations with Africans, Walter and I had come to realize that one of their greatest needs today—and perhaps at the same time the greatest contribution the Christian Church can make to Africa—is for help in the realm of home and family life.

We both knew that many books had been written *about* African marriage problems, but rarely *for* African readers. The students hungered for information and education about sex, love, and marriage. So great was the need that Walter began to teach a marriage course to one of the upper classes.

I helped him by teaching the girl students as he taught the

boys. The eagerness and gratitude with which the classes were received, as well as the many personal talks Walter had with his students and visitors from outside, indicated that here was an open door for future work in Africa.

It was at this time that Walter thought of putting something down in writing that would aid his students. Giving continually the same answers to the same questions was both time and energy consuming. Wouldn't it be more practical to have a small book he could give to those in need of help?

At the same time he was involved in an extensive correspondence with one of his former students who lost his position as a teacher in a mission school because he had become involved with a girl. This young man wrote to Walter in protest, claiming that because no one had paid the bride-price for that girl, he had harmed no one. After a long exchange of letters, the young man gradually received a new outlook on the relationship between sex and love and a new vision of what true marriage is. But when he then met another girl whom he really loved in the deepest sense of the word, her father demanded such a high sum of money as the first installment for the bride-price that the boy was furious. He wrote an angry letter to Walter, protesting this custom and accusing the African fathers of cruel exploitation of their sons, more cruel than the colonization by the whites.

Since the questions treated in this correspondence were asked by many and the complaint which the young man raised in the last letter was the same cry which thousands of young Africans have today, Walter asked his friend whether he would agree to publish this correspondence under a pseudonym.

He agreed. Using this material as a basis, Walter then prepared a small book in his spare time—mostly late at night or early in the morning. Since he intended to use it for his personal counseling ministry, he did not even offer it to a publisher, but printed it privately with the help of a German friend.

How would it be received? The last letter of the young African was left unanswered purposely. Would he succeed in stirring up a nation-wide discussion about the bride-price? Walter hoped for it, because this custom was the main reason for the late marriages of the young men in Cameroun, thereby bringing them into temptation and desperation.

Still we were often downhearted and discouraged. Humanly speaking, the outlook for our work in Cameroun had become somber indeed. Political upheaval and turmoil in the fight for independence had repercussions on our effort to sow the seed.

In a letter to our friends at home we wrote:

"Perhaps it is wholesome that God brings us again and again to our wit's end. The longer one serves on the mission field, the more clearly one realizes how his task, to all outward appearances, approaches impossibility, and even folly. All that is left to us is to cry out: 'Lord, teach us to pray!'

"Only as an answer to prayer can we expect that things will happen in the hearts of our African brethren which will have value for eternity.

"Only as an act of pure grace do we dare to hope that in spite of ourselves and our way of living, the essential message of the Gospel becomes intelligible to the Africans—the message which proclaims the Father of Jesus Christ as the God of the poor, the despised, and the powerless.

"Only as a merciful miracle can it happen that through the fog of Western culture and of all the misunderstandings connected with it, the light of Christ becomes visible."

Sixteen.

On the Slopes of Mount Kilimanjaro

Independence Day came at last to Cameroun on January 1, 1960. In the same month, our third son, Stephen Walter, was born. With his birth on the eve of the anniversary of Vati's death, we experienced once more a light in the darkness of our troubled days.

For many years now I had had the deep desire to write the story of my father's life. I had been collecting material and re-typing his journals, and here in West Africa, Walter and I had literally been walking in his footsteps. But what about his years in Tanganyika, in East Africa? How could I write about that region if I had never visited there?

Libamba was on the western side of Africa, just under the lower edge of the bulge, while Tanganyika was on the east, slightly above South Africa.

That was why, although it was ten years since I first set foot on African soil, I had never visited my father's grave, my own birthplace, the grave of our baby sister Ruth—or any of those scenes that meant so much in the history of our family.

One day I read anew John 16:24: "Hitherto you have asked

nothing in my name; ask, and you will receive, that your joy may be full." On the strength of this promise, I wrote down in my notebook these three petitions:

1. To visit Tanganyika.
2. To have a fifth child.
3. To write my father's story, using his life prayer as a theme: "That Thy Way May be Known."

Only after several weeks did I share these heart petitions with Walter. He listened sympathetically, but then, smiling, he shook his head.

"As if you didn't already have your hands more than full," he said. But he agreed to pray together with me for their fulfillment.

It was now the summer of 1960. A letter from Mother in Bolivia brought us the news that my youngest brother, David, had interrupted his college days long enough to earn money for a trip to South America. She was eagerly awaiting his arrival in La Paz. And then at the end of her letter she wrote:

"John, Adeline, and Veda are urging me to come to Tanganyika when my furlough is due this fall. What do you think about that?"

Of course, we thought it was a wonderful idea and wrote to her right away, urging her to consider it.

For several weeks after that there was no word from her, and I was concerned about what might have happened. She had always written us so regularly.

Imagine our surprise when we received a letter in September addressed to me in Mother's handwriting, but postmarked Capetown, South Africa!

She had decided to take the slightly longer way and go home via Africa. So she sold her typewriter, her few household possessions, and together with what she had saved out of her small missionary allowance, purchased a bus ticket to Rio and from there a boat ticket. David and his Norwegian friend, Sven, had accompanied her across South America to Rio, where they left to return to the States and she boarded the Japanese ship that took her to South Africa.

On September 24 she arrived at Dar es Salaam. There for the first time, seventeen years after the death of her beloved husband, she stood beside his grave. John and Ad had gone to meet her. Afterward they made the two-day trip inland to John's hospital post at Kiomboi, where, too, took place the joyful reunion with Veda.

I was so happy to read her news, but it only increased my desire to visit that part of Africa, too. Tanganyika . . . Kilimanjaro, Dar es Salaam . . . Moshi . . . Mashame—they were the magic words of my childhood. Someday, perhaps when Walter and I retired, I hoped we would see these places. But now, with four little ones—all of them of preschool age . . . It seemed out of the question. And what about the finances? The round-trip plane ticket alone would cost more than five hundred dollars.

Yet, I could only keep on praying: "Ask, and you will receive." A dear friend in Germany encouraged me in this when she sent me a postcard with this inscription on it: "There's only one thing God can't do: Disappoint those who love Him."

Another letter came in November, this time from Tanganyika and again with a surprise: Carl had just arrived unexpectedly from Korea! He had a two-month furlough and would have to be back at his post on January 1. When he had heard that Mother was in Tanganyika, he arranged his travel plans to include a visit there. Mother's joy knew no bounds at having three of her children together even for a short while.

I picked up an unimportant-looking envelope from the pile of mail and opened it absent-mindedly. I took out the folded half sheet of paper it contained. A green check fell out of it. I gasped in astonishment. It was made out to me for the sum of five hundred dollars and was from a giver who wished to remain anonymous. There were only a few words written on the paper:

"For your trip to Tanganyika. You have something to give which I don't have; I have something to give which you don't have. May God use both of our gifts to His Glory!"

I hurried to show it to Walter and Mutti, and they were as excited as I. That evening we had a long conference. It was their idea that I make plans immediately for a trip to Tanganyika, so that I could see Mother and John before they were due to leave in the spring.

"But what about the children?" I asked. "You both have your classes to teach."

"That's why you should leave right away. The day after Christmas," Walter said. "Then we still have two weeks of vacation before the students return. And for two weeks after that we'll manage somehow."

Hildegard Thomas, a German kindergarten teacher who was living with us for the year while she began a kindergarten for the children of the African and European teachers at Libamba, promised that she would help too.

Even Samson, our faithful African houseboy, assured me it would be all right if I left and that he could manage alone the simple meals. "Just write down on a piece of paper what I should cook every day, Madame, and I will do my best," he said.

And so it was decided. I was happy and busy making plans for my trip. Then just before Christmas, a hastily scrawled letter from Veda changed my happiness into apprehension.

John had suffered a heart attack. He was still in serious condition and had been flown from the mission hospital at Kiomboi to the government hospital in Nairobi. Veda had made the flight with him in the Missionary Aviation Fellowship plane, and was sitting by his bedside as she wrote:

"Pray much for him and Adeline in this dark hour. How good it is to have Mother here now when we need her most. She seems to have a gift for being in the right place at the right time. . . ."

Somehow this news made my going more urgent. Even so, on

the eve of my departure my heart was fearful—not only of the long and complicated air trip (I would have to fly over the Congo, possibly even have to land there and this at the time when it was a boiling cauldron), but also at the thought of leaving my family.

It was then that I had a lesson in faith from my five-year-old Kathy. She had taken part in a candle relay race at our station Christmas party. Each participant was to carry a candle from one end of the drafty room to the other without being allowed to shelter the flame. More than once the light blew out and the youngster cautiously had to begin over again.

When it came Kathy's turn, she went without hesitation straight for the goal and hurried back—while the onlookers clapped. The candle burned brighter than ever.

And so I boarded the plane at Yaounde. Five days later I landed safely in Dar es Salaam. I strolled along its beautiful palm-bordered harbor, thinking of my father's lonely walks. I visited the church, right on the waterfront, the same one that he had attended those last months of his life. I ate a noon meal in the modest hotel where he had lived. I sweltered in the sticky heat and felt it sap my energy just as it must have sapped his.

The next morning I went out to the old European cemetery. The only sounds were those of the waves lapping on the shore and of the wind mourning through the trees. I was grateful for the quiet. I wandered among the headstones of missionaries. The graves dated up to the first World War. Dar es Salaam had claimed more than its share of victims. I remembered what one historian had written of this area: "One generation of missionaries after another have sunk into their graves here, but those remaining have stuck to their sweltering stations in faith and out of their sowing in tears has blossomed a noble springtime of God's."

At last I found my way to the new European cemetery. There weren't too many graves here, so I had no trouble finding my father's. It was right beside that of young Pastor Bystrom, who had made the same dangerous crossing of the Atlantic with him, and who had been his successor here. He had died within a few months of my father.

I read the inscription on the simple marble marker:

> RALPH D. HULT
> MISSIONARY PASTOR
> BORN UNITED STATES 1888
> DIED DAR ES SALAAM 1943
> CHRIST IS RISEN

Planted on his grave was an orange African flower—a *gaillard*, as the French call it. Some of its blossoms had gone to seed. In the hard sun-baked earth around the single flower the tiny green shoots were struggling for life. This flower was to me a parable of what Father's life had been.

The next day I talked with the African pastor who knew Ralph Hult best.

"Your father died because of love," he told me, "for it was love that prompted him to make that last safari to the outstations after he got malaria. We were all very sad at his funeral, because one we loved had died. He was one of us. If there was a heavy load to carry—and there were many such loads in the church those days —he always picked up the heaviest end. He never dictated to us. He set us an example."

I wanted to see the European Hospital where my father had spent his last hours. I went to the shore drive and climbed the steps of the arcaded white building.

In the men's ward I asked if I might talk to the oldest "dresser" (male nurse) on the staff. It would be extraordinary to find someone here who might remember what had happened seventeen years ago. But Africans have keen memories. I was taken to meet the oldest nurse. He was a man with a fine-featured, sensitive face.

He smiled in greeting.

"Were you at the hospital in 1943?" I asked him.

"Yes," he said, nodding. "I was working here then."

"My father died in this hospital in March, 1943. Hult was his name, Ralph Hult—"

"Ralph Hult—" he interrupted. "Oh, yes, yes, I knew him. He was a pastor." He looked at me quizzically. "You have the same face as he had. I took care of him. It was I who found him when he died."

"Can you remember which was his room?" I asked.

He thought a minute.

"Yes. It was right here—Number 3. It happens to be empty now. Would you like to see it?"

How much this moment meant to me! He led me into the cool room. Its shaded balcony looked out over the shore drive and the blue Indian Ocean. I felt an atmosphere of restful peace. As I gazed around the room, I could picture it as it had been when he was here. On the bedside table, bare now, I could see his bifocals, his pictures of our family, his watch and pen.

The nurse stretched out both hands to me and enclosed my right hand in his. It was a sign of respect, but more than that, it was a feeling of oneness in compassion.

"I want to thank you for caring for my father in his last days," I said. "You were caring for a man of God. You have a wonderful ministry—all that your hands do for the sick, it is as if they were doing it for Jesus."

He looked puzzled.

"You *are* a Christian, aren't you?" I asked.

"No," he said, "I am a Moslem."

That was how I discovered that the man who had ministered to my father in his last hours was one of those for whom his heart had so long been burdened. I also learned that it was a Hindu who had arranged for an Indian craftsman to carve the inscription on his gravestone. Of those who attended his funeral, only one, a businessman, was an American.

I turned away with thoughtful steps.

But what about John? I had found a letter from Ad upon my arrival in Dar, saying that his condition was about the same, but that his doctor advised an early return to the States.

There was a small mail plane leaving Dar the next morning with stops at Zanzibar, Mombasa, and Nairobi. I arranged for passage on it and called Ad long distance at the mission home in Nairobi to tell her of my plans.

"Where's Mother?" I asked.

"She just left this morning with one of our missionaires for the two-day car trip to Veda's station. She didn't know what your plans were and thought you'd probably be coming there first."

The plane lost altitude for the landing at Nairobi. In the fields below I could see herds of wild antelope and zebra. These were the famous game reserves of Kenya.

During the landing formalities I was startled to hear my name over the loudspeaker. A voice was telling me to go to the information desk. There I found a message: "Proceed to Sadler House Air Terminal. Someone will meet you there." Probably Ad, I thought.

The airport bus drove into Nairobi, the largest city in East Africa, on a route which led through the game reserves. After debilitating days and nights at sea level, the clear, crisp air of the mile-high city brought new life pulsing through me.

As I alighted from the bus with my hand baggage, someone called "Ingrid!"

"Mother!" I gasped in astonishment. Then I was enveloped in her welcoming arms. It was three and a half years since she had left us at the airport in Minneapolis, bound for her second term in Bolivia.

We both began to talk at once. There was so much on which to catch up.

"How is John?" I asked first of all.

"He seems better today," she said. "He's so glad he can see you before they leave for home."

"But how did you get here? When I called Ad yesterday, she said you were on your way to Iramba-land."

"I was. But just as we were leaving Nairobi, I felt I wanted to call Ad once more to get the latest report on John, since I knew she would be back from the hospital at noon. She told me about your change in plans. So I just turned around and came back to Nairobi."

It was from her lips that I learned for the first time the details of my brother's serious illness. In the afternoon, as we went to visit John at the hospital, this is what she told me:

John had been slow in recovering from a severe attack of infectious hepatitis. He made a joke of it, writing us that he and the children (Ad, happily, escaped) hadn't had a white Christmas, but a yellow one. That was a year ago. In his weakened condition, he fell an easy prey to malaria. And as doctors are prone to do when there are cries for help, he went back to work before he had fully recovered.

The following October had been an especially hard month for him because his co-worker was gone part of the time to attend an important medical conference. At night after an already busy day, he was often called back to the hospital in an emergency.

Once three successive operations kept him on duty until eight in the morning.

This is what happened on another day: In the morning he performed four cataract operations, removed an ovarian cyst, and treated a broken arm. He devoted the afternoon to an African with a severe case of tetanus. That evening as John was dressing to go to the Halloween party at the station—it was a big event for the sixty children at the American school—he was called to the hospital. A man, brought in with a strangulated hernia, was near death. It was a difficult case, for the man's relatives had waited too long to carry him in. For six hours John worked over him, repairing the damage. The man would recover, but the next week John had a heart attack.

Meanwhile, Mother and Veda had gone on a few days' vacation trip up to the Kilimanjaro area in northern Tanganyika. They had just returned to Veda's station at Iambi in time to hear the evening radio messages between the mission stations.

They listened apprehensively as a voice called for the Missionary Aviation Fellowship plane to come down from Nairobi. Then they heard the request to pick up John, and the news that he had suffered a severe heart attack during the night. The doctor wanted to get him to the government hospital at Nairobi as soon as possible.

What a shock for Veda and Mother! They made plans to go at once by jeep to Kiomboi. If John were in serious condition, he would need a nurse to accompany him on the flight. Why not his own sister?

The day after the flight Mother, who had stayed behind at Kiomboi, received a telegram from Veda:

"GOOD FLIGHT. JOHN RESTING QUIETLY. TEST EXAMINATION TODAY."

The doctor found a coronary condition and ordered complete bed rest. He advised John to return to the States as soon as possible. So Veda went back to her work at the Leprosarium and Ad to pack their belongings, while Mother went to Nairobi and stayed with John. He would remain hospitalized until the day of his flight to the States, and she was happy to be with him at a time of need.

As I listened to Mother's account I realized that nearly four years had elapsed since we said good-by to John in Minneapolis. It is strange how it is with close families. They may not see each other for years on end, yet the minute they meet again, the years melt away as if they had never been.

John was thinner and had a few more lines in his face, but otherwise he looked the same to me. We enjoyed some good moments together, comparing notes on West and East Africa.

Later, Mother and I went to make the family's air reservations. We were happy to learn that they would not be returning to the States alone, for whom did we meet at the airplane counter book-ing passage on the same flight but "Uncle Lud" Melander. "Uncle Lud" was like a member of our family. A confirmed bachelor, he had served as a missionary in Tanganyika for almost forty years and accompanied Father on his trip to Victoria Falls. But we had seen him from time to time on his visits to America. His hair was white now, but he was still apple-cheeked. He carried his beloved violin as usual under his arm.

"Uncle Lud" introduced us to his wife, Esther, who had been a fellow passenger on the ill-fated *Zamzam* with Father. We were happy that "Uncle Lud" had not remained single.

The day of John's departure came. We got to the airport just as the flight to Paris was being called. A hasty farewell, and the little party disappeared through the gate.

It was almost two years since Veda came to see us at Libamba. Now it was my turn to visit her with Mother in her African home. During the week I was with her, I had the chance to observe the work she was doing as head nurse of the Iambi Leprosarium where five hundred patients were cared for in Christian love. The leprosarium had been carefully planned by Dr. Stanley Moris as a model for up-to-date treatment. I often walked with Veda as she went on her rounds in the spotless hospital wards.

One day she introduced me to a male patient. He was sightless, and had only stumps for hands.

"How are you today?" Veda asked in Swahili.

"I have awakened in good health. There's nothing wrong with me," he answered.

Veda said to me softly after we had passed him:

"It always gives me a lift to hear him express his thankfulness. He has so little, it seems, to be thankful for—not even a relative who cares for him."

The days with Veda were rich ones for me. The night before I left, I realized how hard it would be to say good-by. She would be alone now, for Mother was returning with me to Libamba for a short visit. I thought of Veda as I opened my journal, and of the two wonderful girls, Lois and Lore, with whom she lived. There were others like them, too, scattered at lonely stations throughout the world. I wrote:

"These noble single workers—how shall I describe them? They're women, all of them, but they're supposed to do the work of men. Of course they're weak; after all, they're women. But they can't afford to be weak. They must hide their feelings behind an armor of self-protection. They have to handle jeeps, driving through roads where there's no bottom, or cowpaths where there are no markers. They have to hoist boxes and barrels, build outstations, deliver babies, organize leprosy patients, perform a hundred tasks for which they are not fitted by nature. But if they fail somewhere along the way, they are subjected to merciless criticism. All of them would prefer the calling of home and family, yet they are here because they have been obedient to God's call, and He has entrusted them with this great task. God has chosen the weak things of the world that He might put to shame them that are strong. It's proof to me of God's power as I see the work of these noble ones."

Before leaving Iambi, a letter from Walter brought heartwarming news. The first printing of his booket, *J'ai aimé une fille* (*I Loved a Girl*), was completely sold out after having been on sale only six weeks in Yaounde. He had sent sample copies of it to his friends in other African countries and already there were several requests for the translation rights. But the most unexpected result was an avalanche of letters from African readers.

Since the booklet itself was the correspondence between Walter and his young friend, the readers had evidently drawn the conclusion that Walter must be someone who not only reads letters and takes them seriously, but who answers them too. So why couldn't he solve their problems as well? The letters came from all corners of Cameroun and all walks of life, sharing intimate personal problems and revealing an urgent and unanswered need.

Many of these letters, Walter said, came from those who had never been in touch with Christianity.

So he had begun to prepare a second French edition for the other French-speaking countries of Africa, as well as an English edition for the English-speaking African countries. It was clear now that we were on the threshold of a new ministry.

I could hardly wait to get back to Libamba. With a song of rejoicing in our hearts, Mother and I set out for Nairobi and the return trip.

But first came the stop at Moshi, in the area where Mother and Father had once been stationed. It was after dark when we arrived, so our first glimpse of Mount Kilimanjaro was delayed until morning. We saw it then from our bedroom window—"The Shining Mountain," as it was called in Swahili—proud and silent, glistening in the morning sun. We were guests in the home of the Danielsons. This was the same Mrs. Danielson who had been on the *Zamzam* with her six children. Now the youngest, brown-eyed Lois Christine, would also be coming to Tanganyika as a missionary upon completion of a year of special training.

Pastor Danielson arranged for a car to take us up the west side of the mountain to Mashame, a distance of twenty miles. There was a rapt expression on Mother's face. At every turn in the mountain road, memories came rushing back to her: of her first trip up here in a contraption called a monowheel, a sort of chair built over a motorcycle wheel, with one man pushing and another pulling. Little Paul was with her then. He was not quite a year old and had to be carried in a hammock. Father rode on a donkey. She even recalled the name of her old cook, Nderasiya. Leaning forward, she asked our driver if he knew him.

"Yes," he answered. "His home is just around the next curve."

We requested him to stop. What a look of unbelieving joy when Nderasiya first caught sight of "Mama Hulti"!

He took flower petals and scattered them in the path for Mother to walk on. He ran into his house, came out with a bench over which he carefully spread his best robe, and asked her to be seated. Then he brought her a gift of eggs and bananas and ten shillings.

With this money—a very large amount for him—she was to go to a restaurant on her journey and eat while thinking of him.

Mother explained to me that she had cared for his infant niece after her mother had died. This little girl was said to be the first baby of her tribe to have survived the death of a mother in childbirth. "It was not long after that," Mother said, "that I lost my own baby, Ruth Eleanor. Nderasiya has been faithful. For thirty-seven long years now, he has unfailingly tended little Ruth's grave."

Not only had he been my parents' first cook in Tanganyika, but he had also served as my father's guide and interpreter on his long treks.

Nderasiya had even been along when in 1924 Father, with another missionary, made the trip of investigation to Iramba-land. It had taken them, Mother said, six hard days of walking to cover the same ground we'd done yesterday in a half day. Mother remembered that when Father came back from that trip, his worn-out shoes were bound to his feet by wire.

We took our leave of Nderasiya. It was wonderful for me to be sharing this pilgrimage with Mother. The car in which we were riding rounded the bend now, and we could see the station. A more beautiful spot I could hardly imagine, located as it was in full view of majestic Mount Kilimanjaro. In the background were the tall pine trees which would have been at home in the Black Forest. They had been planted by German missionaries. In the foreground were the brilliant colors of poinsettia, African hibiscus, and other shrubs and plants.

Later in the day, while Mother visited with friends, I stood alone in front of the plain wooden cross that marked my sister's grave. Below were the green slopes of the mountainside covered with the rich coffee and banana plantations of the Chagga. Above, just visible over the tips of the tall pine trees, was "The

Shining Mountain." It was a translucent rose in the moments before sunset. No wonder many Africans preferred to call it by the more awesome name, "The Throne of God." I remained transfixed by the mightiness, by the wonder, of the mountain.

I remembered what Veda had written to us as she climbed to the top together with another missionary nurse during her first term:

"It's only from the mountaintops that we can hope to see the end from the beginning, to catch a glimpse of God's plan and purpose in our lives as we go on our way rejoicing!"

At this moment, too, I was conscious of the nearness of my father. He must have stood on this spot often during those last weeks of his life before he went down to Dar es Salaam to die. Strange that his presence here should be so much stronger than at the sandy grave.

How many of his prayers and dreams have seen fruition since his tired body was laid to rest! I thought of last summer when members of his family had been serving not only at home, but on five continents, fulfilling our family Psalm:

"That thy way may be known upon earth, thy salvation among all nations."

Epilogue

The day was April 20, 1963. Once more it was springtime in the Ozarks. Mother opened the French windows of Bethany Cottage and looked out in the early morning stillness where the rolling acres of the Homestead lay fresh and trim.

Birds were singing in the trees that Father had planted, in the tall Chinese elm which now shaded the front of the house—Carl's tree, planted the day he was born. The jasmine-colored leaves of the Russian olive on the southwest corner of the house—Gus's tree—were in pleasing contrast to the dark green of Marty's elm to the south. There, too, was the tree that Father had planted on Grandmother's seventieth birthday.

Mother looked at the clock on her dresser. In a few minutes Paul's plane would be landing at the Springfield airport. It was a long trip for him to make from Tucson, but he had been so enthusiastic about the plans for the reunion of the ten brothers and sisters that he arranged for time off. John and Ad had already arrived from Denver the night before.

With great thankfulness Mother thought of John. Just two years ago he'd had the heart attack in Tanganyika and was flown home. He had made a slow but complete recovery; he was now busy with his own practice as a pediatrician in Denver. He was the tenor soloist in the choir of the large Augustana church there. She smiled as she remembered that he had sung "How Beautiful upon the Mountain are the Feet of Them That Publisheth Good Tidings" when she visited there a few weeks ago. He told her afterward that in his heart he had dedicated it to her.

Mother thought of her other children. Walter and I were already here at the Homestead settled in the cottage "Dar es Salaam" where we would make our furlough headquarters with our five children—no, it was only four children. Mother had offered to take charge of the youngest during the months when I would be concentrating on the writing of the family story. Eighteen-month-old Ruthy was still sleeping peacefully in her crib in the corner of Mother's bedroom. What a strong affinity she felt for this sturdy little granddaughter of hers, whose golden curls bobbed up and down with every energetic step she took. It was almost as if, in Ruthy, God had given her back the daughter she had lost in Africa so many years ago.

Walter, too, was busy writing *I Love a Young Man*, the sequel to *I Loved a Girl*. He hoped to finish it soon. Almost unbelievable was the enthusiastic response from readers of the first book. Already he was corresponding with Africans from nineteen different countries, and there were requests for translation rights from both Asia and South America. Even young people in the United States were finding it helpful and were writing him letters of appreciation.

Mother's thoughts were interrupted by the sound of a car coming up the drive. Max and Martha! She ran to the door to welcome them. They'd driven all night from Illinois and said that Vince and Eunie with their five children would be arriving soon too. Just then Carl came out of his room, rubbing his eyes sleepily. He embraced Marty warmly, and she told him how much better he was looking now, than when he had arrived home from Korea a few weeks earlier. He grinned and showed her the blisters on his hands from chopping down trees. Then he showed her the field he had plowed for Mother's garden.

After breakfast came the most spectacular arrival of all—a red station wagon with all the Hults from Minneapolis: David, now a senior at the University of Minnesota; Mary, a nurse at Fairview Hospital; Gus and Maria, doing social work there; and Veda, home on leave from Tanganyika.

For the first time in more than twenty years Mother had her ten children gathered around her at the Homestead. Playing happily and noisily under the trees were also twelve of her twenty-four grandchildren.

The day passed quickly. Walks in the woods, a ball game, a picnic supper on the lawn, and then the family gathered once more in the living room of Bethany Cottage. Almost instinctively we began to sing the old songs of our childhood: "Children of the Heavenly Father," "Day is Dying in the West," "Jesus, Tender Shepherd, Hear Me."

"Children," she asked, "what would you think if I accept this position and settle down once more in Bethany Cottage where five of you were born?"

We all raised both hands to show our double unanimity.

Walter read then from the last prayer of Jesus with His disciples in John 17:21: "That they may all be one . . . that the world may believe that thou hast sent me." He explained that in Germany it is the custom of the Moravian Brethren to celebrate the Lord's Supper together just as Jesus had done it with His disciples —by passing the cup from one to the other and then the bread— all seated in a circle. In the intimacy of our family circle it could be done in the same way—each one passing the cup of communion to the one at the right and sharing with him at the same time a personal Word of God.

This was a deeply meaningful experience. It reminded me how strong were our family bonds, that regardless of what the future held, they would remain unbroken. And the story would not end. Perhaps it had only begun.

*   *   *   *   *

The day is April 2o, 1976. As I sit writing again, it is not springtime in the Ozarks, but in the mountains of Austria, for Walter and I now live in a small Alpine village close to Salzburg. Our five children, now of high school and college age, enjoy living in the "Sound of Music" country.

Twelve years have passed since this book was first published. All of my brothers and sisters are now married and currently living in the United States. John made a good recovery from his heart attack and is serving as a pediatrician among the underprivileged children in Denver, Colorado. Veda is a busy pastor's wife in Minnesota. Eunice and Vince are living in Springfield, Missouri, where Vince is pastor of Immanuel Church, built on the Homestead grounds.

Walter's mother, Mutti, made her home with us until she passed away in 1967.

Ingred's mother, now seventy-seven, makes her home in Springfield, Missouri. She is in good health and active in all the work of Immanuel congregation, in addition to being grandmother to more than thirty grandchildren and four great-grandchildren. It was a great joy for her last summer to have all ten of her children, plus their spouses, as well as almost all of her children's children together for the long weekend of the Fourth of July at our old home. For all fifty of us it was a time of celebration as we became conscious again of the unity of spirit and rich heritage God has entrusted to us.

As I sit at my desk and write these lines in our little mountain home, I remember the strong feeling I had twelve years ago as I finished writing this book: "The story would not end. Perhaps it had only begun." When I wrote in the last chapter that Walter and I were "on the threshold of a new ministry," none of us could have dreamed just how true this feeling was!

Our new ministry has grown out of Walter's book *I Loved a Girl,* and it is still growing. Walter often says, "First I wrote the book. Now it is writing our lives."

I Loved a Girl went around the world. Requests for translations have reached us from all continents and we now have more than seventy translations and editions of the book on a shelf in our living room. It is read by the Chinese and well as the Eskimos. There are Hebrew and Arabic translations, as well as a braille and Esperanto edition. It has appeared in all major European languages, including five languages behind the Iron Curtain. The book has evidently touched the nerve of a worldwide problem.

The result has been an avalanche of personal letters from readers, asking for help with their family problems. We consider it a part of our ministry to faithfully answer these letters as time and strength allows.

Out of this ministry of correspondence another one has grown. Invitations have reached us from churches and other Christian organizations around the world to conduct what we call "Family Life Seminars."

We have been back to Cameroun three times, visiting our first home in Tcholliré where we found the young church flourishing, faithfully supporting more than one hundred outposts in the midst of great hardship.

At the present time we again have the definite impression that we are not experiencing an end, but rather another new beginning. We have been led far beyond our original field in Cameroun to Liberia, Ethiopia, Kenya, Tanzania, South Africa, and even beyond the continent of Africa to Indonesia, New Caledonia, and the greatest island of the world, New Guinea, near Australia.

Maybe some readers would like to know what happens in such a Family Life Seminar. Here is a description as we experienced it in the summer of 1975 in New Guinea:

Imagine fifteen couples sitting on the floor in a simple room. The babies sleep, or are nursed or rocked in a net which the mothers carry on their heads. The bishop and his wife, the district president, nurses, teachers, pastors, and theological students are among the participants, as well as simple villagers and fishermen.

Besides the deepening of the spiritual life of husband and wife, and teaching about all aspects of marriage, it is one of the major goals of our seminars to practice communication. On the first day each husband has to shake hands with his wife. Some are unable to do it. They are asked to practice in their rooms all by themselves. The next day they can do it with more ease. Then we practice looking at each other. First the men among themselves, then the women, and finally each couple.

The third day we can start to practice talking. Each one has to think of three things he especially likes about his partner. After a time of quiet reflection, the couples go outside, one by one, and sit down together facing each other. Each husband has to tell his wife, each wife her husband these three things in their mother tongue. Some need more than an hour before they finish.

The following day, the couples may volunteer to share with the group what they have told each other. To our surprise they were very willing to do this. Evidently what they appreciated most about each other was reliability. This was mentioned time and again. In such a time of change—New Guinea became independent the sixteenth of September 1975—there seemed to be an overwhelming need to have someone upon whom one could depend. We shall never forget a young teacher, who reminded us of an Assyrian warrior, with his dark eyes, aquiline nose, and magnificent black beard. He sat down with his wife in the center of the group circle and said to her, "I love you because you do not want me to die, for you give me to eat." Then he could not hold back his tears of joy that he had been able to verbalize his feelings.

It is strange, but evidently the feeling of being loved can only enter through the ear. Maybe some of our readers would like to try telling someone close what you like about them? It is certainly a good feeling to be loved, and you don't have to travel to New Guinea for such an experience.

Ingrid's messages during these seminars can be found in her book *The Joy of Being a Woman,* and Walter's lectures are contained in his book *I Married You.* This book describes four action-packed days in an African city, as we have experienced them again and again.

Have we forsaken our original missionary call? Those who read *I Married You* will find the answer there. We strongly believe that family life work is one of the most promising doors for proclaiming the Gospel of Jesus Christ to modern man.

In the developing countries, an interaction is taking place; on one hand the conflicts arising out of the situation of rapid social change cause the people to open up to the message of the Gospel. On the other hand, only the Gospel provides help in depth for the ones suffering from these conflicts. No marriage can be helped unless husband and wife come to a personal encounter with Jesus Christ. This is why witness and serving are interrelated in our work.

Our own Mission Board in Minneapolis advised us to make provision for an organizational structure of our work which would correspond to its special history, growth, and outreach. In order to underline the unity of word and deed when proclaiming the Gospel, we have chosen the three internationally known words FAMILY LIFE MISSION to design our activities (lectures, seminars, literature, radio programs, correspondence). We conceive of this work as MISSION because we believe that the renewal of the FAMILY is possible only through the One Who has said, "I am the LIFE."

"FLM" is an independent, interdenominational, nonprofit organization mainly supported through private gifts. It is a fellowship of those who have recognized family life work as a missionary task. It operates through a steering committee in Germany in cooperation with the Mission Department of the Bavarian Church.

Our call has not changed—only its dimension.

> Ingrid Hult Trobisch —
> A-4880 St. Georgen
> Austria